Unconventional Voyages

Unconventional Voyages

Arthur Lower

Author of Colony To Nation *Etc., Etc.*

THE RYERSON PRESS · TORONTO

Published October, 1953

PRINTED AND BOUND IN CANADA
BY THE RYERSON PRESS, TORONTO

TO E. M. L.
Shipmate and Unconventional Voyageuse

Foreword

I BEGAN to make these sketches because I thought I had had a few experiences which lent themselves to literary treatment. I went on with them because they began to recall to me so vividly certain aspects of my life. They are just a few of the many that I might have included.

I suppose I have always lived a double life: by winter an academic and in the summers, reverting to some form of the primitive. It is the primitive, not the sophisticated, that draws me back to the scenes and occasions I try to tell about in these pages—the primitive as represented by the forest and the sea.

Despite their nearness to the forest, few Canadians seem to understand how close these two are, forest and sea. This country was explored from the thwarts of the birch canoe. Even today much of our north country is still dependent on improved versions of the same perfect invention. In my days in the north, and it must still be in large measure the same, no one thought of walking—except from the campfire to his blankets. There was nowhere to walk! The only pathways were the rivers and lakes, and the rivers and lakes led everywhere. So to be in the north, in the bush, was to be in a canoe and upon the water.

From the canoe to the deck of a ship is not such a large jump as might be thought: it is not nearly so large a jump as from the deck of a ship to a canoe! Many of our Canadian lads have made it and have felt at home on the heaving sea five minutes after they have got there. Among others, I made this jump, and in doing so must have reached some previous familiar existence, so congenial was the world of waters to me.

It has been a pretty good life, this combination of the erudite with the primitive. Each has reflected back upon the other. I am sure I am a better scholar because I know the bush and the sea, because I can split wood, make a bough bed, snare a rabbit, run a rapids, reef a sail, tie a bowline and shape a course. My sea service, the acquaintance it gave me with navigation, has come in singularly handy for studies in history and geography: it has helped enormously in the appreciation of the strategic problems of our times. My canoe trips have made the lives and deeds of the original explorers and discoverers infinitely more alive for me than if I had known no more about such matters than one learns out of books. Even my limited acquaintance with our Indians and their language has stood me in good stead in various corners of my professional work.

So I am glad that I have had this combination, the simple and the sophisticated. It is one still open in peculiar degree to Canadians, if they still have the good sense to take advantage of it. For nothing can eliminate our frontier, that vast land to the north there, just beyond our glance, a land which the airplane may fly over but will never subordinate. We Canadians will always have this northern window through which to let fresh air into our civilized room. If we heap ourselves up in festering cities, that will be partly our own fault—for just beyond their pavement's end, stands the open, unfenced north. And if we can ever produce a way of life in this country which will be uniquely our own, it will arise from this combination of the simple and the sophisticated, from the complex skills and worldly wisdom of an urban civilization joined to the heritage of space and the clear untroubled eyes of a world which is eternally young.

And as to the sea! Is it not eternally young also? Is it not a frontier, too, which calls out all the resources and ingenuity and adaptiveness of man? Happy the men—of whom I have been one—who have known both frontiers.

> "The sea, the sea, the open sea,
>   The bright, the blue, the ever free!"

But don't forget the forest where real, not synthetic Hiawathas are still practising their craft.

> I a light canoe will build me
> Build a swift Chemaun for sailing
> That shall float upon the river
> Like a yellow leaf in Autumn
> Like a yellow water lily.

Horizon House,
July 26, 1953.   A. R. M. L.

Contents

I

Storm-Stayed on Lake Simcoe

I DON'T know where the drop of seafaring blood came from that got into my veins. Certainly not from forebears that I know anything about, all of whom seem to have confined themselves strictly to safe city streets. I suppose I should partially except my father from that statement: when he came to Canada as a young man, he was induced to settle in a little town on the shores of an inland lake, one of those lesser lakes of ours that would be a great lake in any country which did not have such a store of greater ones. Part of the inducement, I have always understood, was the lake. Yet he never had a foothold of his own on its shore, for other Englishmen, Englishmen of the "huntin', shootin' and fishin'" variety had got there before him and pre-empted all the good sites.

But they could not pre-empt Lake Simcoe. On it and in it, the boys of my town and generation were brought up: we began our acquaintance with the outdoor life at an early age.

One summer when I was about eleven years old, my family was "camping" down at Big Bay Point. My brother and my brother-in-law, in the course of their holidays, decided to try the fishing over at Fox Island. There were no motorboats in those days, and those who know the locality will recall that Fox Island stands well out in the lake from Big Bay Point. As I recall it, to get there involved a row of several miles down the shore and then a plunge of three miles or so out to the island across the open lake. Lake Simcoe is not to be trifled with, and my elders and betters probably should have had sense enough not to attempt a trip like that in a small rowboat. My parents were not there at the time or the expedition would probably have been vetoed. As it was, the two young men, in holiday mood, decided to take a chance, planning to set out early in the morning and come back the same evening. Their plans did not include a small boy as passenger, but he vigorously protested his rights and in the end was allowed to go.

We were off shortly after sunrise. To this day I can see the blue sheen of the lake, glassy still and reflecting the pink morning clouds, the far York county shore just visible over to the southwest and out beyond it, the clean rim of the horizon. It being so calm, we struck straight for the island, passing the big shoal that lies half-way between but not daring to try our luck there, for fear of wind. We got to Fox Island without adventure, and did a little fishing in the neighbourhood. Then after lunch it came on to blow from the northwest, and we pulled in. There was a lighthouse on the island in those days and, more to the point, a lighthouse-keeper. This old man lived there all summer by himself, so he was always glad to see visitors.

The island was quite unspoiled, as I remember it, and absolutely full of the most tempting chokecherries that the mind of youth ever imagined. It had a reputation for snakes, but I cannot recall seeing any.

Towards evening the wind had risen still higher and made it quite out of the question for us to return to Big Bay Point. The lighthouse-keeper invited us to stay the night. This was not so good for my brother-in-law, who had left his wife behind him to do the worrying, in the full knowledge that she would. But it was pure

Paradise for a boy of eleven. I remember going up with the keeper to light up. He even interrupted an important card game for the purpose. "The light must be lit," he said; "in all the fifteen (or was it fifty?) years I've been here, that light's always been lit." This seemed like sheer heroism to me at the time, but years later it occurred to me that he had nothing else to do with his time, anyway.

The lighthouse registers in my memory—and I am sure it loses nothing by the lapse of time—as something vast and high, so high that it meant a lengthy and exciting climb up numerous ladders to get to the light. After dark, the wind rumbled round it in satisfactory disconsolate manner and, inside, the lamplight cast flickering rays over wooden beams in the most conventionally romantic fashion. The lighthouse had an extra bunk or two, and, stowed in one of these, I was soon asleep. It was heaven to drop off amid all this grandeur.

The next day the nor'wester was still blowing. I have learned a good deal about nor'westers since then. If they come up and blow all night, as this one had, they will certainly blow all the next day and probably a good part of the third day, too. If you have only a small boat, there is no remedy for them but patience.

Sure enough, the wind did blow all the next day, whipping up a sea round the corner of the island that would have made short work of our little skiff. I cannot say that I was displeased. Long before the mature age of eleven I had gorged myself on good old Captain Collingwood and his mate, W. H. G. Kingston, with their narrow escapes at sea, their castings-up on desert islands and their bloody naval battles, so this desert island was right up my alley, especially as there seemed no lack of food and a complete absence of "savages." The day passed very acceptably and as it ended, I again went up to see that the lamp was properly lighted. I remember very distinctly hearing a fag-end of conversation as I dropped off that

evening. "They was fine fellows," the lighthouse-keeper
was saying, "here three days. And when they left, blessed
if they didn't go and put some money on the table when
I wasn't lookin'."

The wind was still blowing hard on the second
morning, but not with the sweep of the previous afternoon. It had got to the stage of vicious thrusts, with lulls
between. A council of war produced the decision to wait
until after lunch and then "try it."

After lunch there was still a good deal of wind, but
opinion seemed to be that we could "make it," so we
put off.

The moment we got out of the shelter of the island
it became very problematical indeed if we could "make
it." We had three miles or more to row before we got a
lee, and right in the teeth of the wind. The two men
were rowing and I was encouraging them from the stern.
They pulled around to the exposed side of the island and
decided to lay up again. Running ashore, with the waves
behind us, we got a little wet, so began to make a fire.

At that point, before the match had been lighted, a
miracle occurred. No ordinary miracle either, but a
sudden beautiful act of heaven, breath-taking in its
unexpectedness, its clarity and its completely satisfactory
nature. Around the point of the island there appeared,
or so it seemed to me—a ship, under full sail! I was surely
back in Elizabethan times, standing by to board the
Spanish galleon. The ship came grandly about on to the
starboard tack. By this time she was closer and had got
a little smaller. In fact she had shrunk to a schooner, and
to one that we all recognized, one that was, in fact, hired
out by the week. But I had had my grand moment of
illusion, and I shall keep it until the end of my life. I
can still see that good, green stem cutting the waves in
gallant style, the jib let go, the fore and main swinging
over and the helmsman running her off the wind down

along the shore opposite to where our boat was drawn up. They waved to us, and we put out to them. They told us that they were going over to the Simcoe county shore and would take us over. So we got aboard, and they took our skiff in tow.

It was my very first experience of sail. I was enchanted with the swift motion of the boat through the water, that smoothness of motion which the wind alone can impart, the slash of the waves across the bow, and the general air of alertness and subdued efficient excitement of everybody on board. Not for nothing had I learned from my school reader:

> Ho, breakers on the weather bow
> And hissing white the sea!
> About the good ship goes, and leaves
> Old England on the lea!

The main shore came up all too soon. It was probably only a matter of an hour or so, to beat in against that spanking breeze, but it seemed to me like a deep-sea voyage. Upon me there had been put a mark.

The rest, I am afraid, was anticlimax. We pulled laboriously back to Big Bay Point, in the shelter of the shore, rather hungry, without any fish that I can remember, and, I suppose, the two men very conscious of the worry they were causing to the womenfolk. This, when we got ashore, I discovered to my amazement. My sister was quite sure that her husband had been drowned, whatever had become of her two brothers. For my part, I couldn't understand how anyone could do anything but rejoice over two nights in a lighthouse, two days marooned on a desert island, all finished up with as gallant and spanking a voyage as Drake ever made in his quest of the Spaniards' doubloons.

II

The "Mariposa Belle"

READERS of Stephen Leacock will recall that one of his *Sunshine Sketches* tells of the sinking of the *Mariposa Belle,* a small steamer on an inland lake. He gives a playful account of an excursion, hitting off with skill the various local characters who are on board and managing to convey through them the impression that, for pure adventure, the excursion ranks with an expedition to the South Seas. At a critical point an emergency arises and the ship begins to sink. Amid scenes of terror she settles slowly down. Yet hope flickers when a boat is sighted, pulling frantically from the shore. The rescuer draws nearer and nearer. Unfortunately, by the time he reaches her, the *Mariposa Belle* has settled to the bottom. It is only a Leacockian tragedy, however, for the water proves but a few feet in depth and the little boat sits comfortably on the mud. As for the rescuer, he puts so much zeal into his effort that when he comes alongside, he is done for, and it is not the shipwrecked passengers who must be rescued, but the rescuer.

Leacock's good-humoured satire signalizes the passing of an epoch—that period between the early pioneer days and our modern urban civilization, when the primitive methods of getting about had been superseded and the ubiquitous gas engine had not come in. It was pre-eminently the age of steam, and by the steam engine,

6

installed in anything that would float, the back-country of Ontario was opened up. All the way along The Front, as the shores of the St. Lawrence and the lower lakes were termed, settlement worked back into the bush, supported by steamers wherever lake or river allowed them.

These little inland steamers might be anything—ambitious boasts or hardly more than scows with engines. For two generations or more, or until the seventies, when the interior railway system of the Province had become fairly complete, they carried the goods, the crops, the animals and the persons of the people in the back townships. After the railways displaced them as common carriers, they were used for pleasure traffic and tried to keep going by means of "excursions." The period of the "excursion steamer" on the secondary waters of Ontario lasted from about 1880 until 1910 or 1915. By the latter year, the internal combustion engine was putting automobiles on the roads and gasoline launches on the water. Everybody could then make his own "excursion" and the steamer rapidly lost its customers.

Many of these little boats when they ceased to pay, were tied up to wharves and they and the wharf rotted away together. Others burned, but it remained for one to achieve the distinction, if not of being shipwrecked, at least of sinking.

That one was the original of the *Mariposa Belle*. Her name was the *Enterprise*.

Leacock was an Orillian, and being such, was, as every citizen of the neighbouring and fairer town of Barrie knows, capable of appropriating any of the unconsidered trifles of the region and building them into the greater glory of his own home town. The true centre of light in Simcoe County, however, was the county town, Barrie. There, Lake Simcoe was to be seen at its best; the long reach of Kempenfelt Bay, blue in the sunshine, with the clear line of the horizon opening out at its end, contrasted sharply with the shallow limestone basin, Lake Couchiching, beside which Orillia was built. In those days, neither town had a literary man to celebrate it, but when Leacock, on his way to fame, came out with his *Sunshine Sketches,* he made up for lost time. Since then, Orillia has never ceased to pat itself on the back for being the sleepy little town of his sketches.

Orillians apparently will pat themselves on the back at the slightest provocation, for if anyone should suggest to them that their town really is sleepy, he would be run out. This egregious place, not far from the wilderness of the Canadian Shield, grew up as a "jumping off point" for the bush; it has never entirely lost the marks of its origin. To this day, I am told, it is full of effervescent, incandescent people who form the strongest possible contrast to their dignified and stable neighbours in Barrie. Anxious to stand in the spotlight, however slender its claims to that position, Orillia, I learn, has sought to add to its fame as a sleepy little town the purely accidental renown of a visit from the great Champlain. It is possible that the explorer passed through the "Narrows" (where Lake Simcoe empties into Lake Couchiching) on his way from the Georgian Bay to the Bay of Quinte, but that seems hardly sufficient reason for erecting a pretentious monument to him on a spot in which he could have had no interest whatsoever. Citizens of Barrie would not erect a monument to the Angel Gabriel, even if a visit from him should actually have taken place. They are their own best monuments, and feel no need of support from men like Champlain. Had Leacock lived in Barrie, he would, as a native son, have been ostentatiously ignored.

In view of the foregoing and in common justice to Barrie, the history of the *Mariposa Belle* incident should be set down correctly.

During the steamboat age, the jealousy between the two towns naturally extended to the boats which plied from them. Orillia's pride was the *Islay,* and toward her, Barrieites showed scant respect. Their favourite was the *Enterprise,* a noble bluff-bowed old lady that pushed half the lake along in front of her and covered everyone with cinders when she came in to the wharf. Between supporters of the rival vessels, two major points were under frequent discussion. One related to the question of speed. It was rumoured that the *Islay* could do ten knots (though few knew exactly what a "knot" was), and alleged that the *Enterprise* could do only nine. As against this, there were eye-witness accounts of how the *Enterprise* had won races, as it were, by a nose. Considerable reliance was also placed on logic: the *Enterprise* had two engines, was actually twin-screwed, like a liner. That should have settled it.

The other contentious matter concerned seaworthiness. The inhabitants of the shores of Lake Simcoe were, in the mass, a good deal more familiar with the plough than with the deck of a ship, and in consequence, if they found themselves farther from the shore than the distance you could throw a stone, they became apprehensive. The average excursionist sought above all else placid water and safety. Any minor mishap, such as a little engine trouble, was sufficient to ruin a boat's reputation, for, if such things could happen, she could not be safe. Every excursionist, with certain bold exceptions—persons looked on as not entirely normal, such as the rector whom Leacock depicts (I remember that he was not entirely normal)— went on the waters of Lake Simcoe with a delightful sense of dangerous adventure. On one occasion, a small steamer, caught in a wind between Snake and Fox Islands, began to roll, and the passengers, terrified, called on the Reverend Mr. Blank, who happened to be among them,

to lead in prayer. He did so, and they all sang "For
Those in Peril on the Sea." Lake Simcoe was no ordinary
lake, and the ships that ploughed it, no ordinary ships.
The flat, round *Enterprise,* it was felt, compared with the
long sneaky *Islay,* was definitely "safe."

Where these two boats went for the winter, the small
boys of Barrie could never discover, but for those boys,
it used to be the great event of the year when word went
round in the spring that a steamer was coming up the bay.
If she should prove to be the *Islay,* that was taken as no
great matter, for she was only an old boat from Orillia,
but if it were the *Enterprise,* then, indeed, worth had
triumphed.

The incident which Leacock purloined for Orillia in
connection with his *Mariposa Belle,* occurred in the
summer of 1902. The actual facts I here recount.

In the early August of that summer, I was a member
of the group of young savages camping down at Big Bay
Point, where Kempenfelt Bay joins the open lake. We
had, for the first time in our lives, shaken free of our
parents, and were shifting, quite satisfactorily, for ourselves. Yet I was glad to learn one day that my mother
was coming down from Barrie on the *Enterprise* and that
I was to go with her over to Jackson's Point, and return.
It was by no means my first trip across the lake, for my
earliest memories were of such expeditions. So Big Bay
Point, Jackson's Point, Belle Ewart, Roche's Point, were
familiar excursion calls to me from earliest days.

On this particular trip, I duly met my mother, and we
went across the lake to Jackson's Point. It was a beautiful
blue and silver day, with not a ripple on the surface. The
ten miles across took about an hour. We had our picnic
supper, got on board again and the boat pulled out.
Returning was as uneventful as going. From Big Bay
Point up to Barrie, the boat cut over to the north shore

of the bay, and kept fairly close in. This was unusual, for crossing the bay instead of taking a direct course added a couple of miles to the length of the trip.

As we came up the bay, we crept closer and closer to the shore. Then, when we reached the town, an extraordinary thing happened. In those days Barrie had two wharves, one, the more easterly, at the foot of Mulcaster Street; the other, invariably used, at the foot of Bayfield Street. The *Enterprise* put in at Mulcaster Street: in a small boy's eyes, this was as though a C.P.R. liner should dock at St. John's, Newfoundland, instead of coming up to Montreal.

The puzzled passengers went ashore. Nothing unusual was observed aboard the boat. But in the morning, there she was, lying at the wharf and sitting on the bottom!

Her bows were up, and the great square doors in them, through which her hawsers came out, made her look like a big dead fish. Her stern was well under. There was no doubt about it. She had sunk!

Within a few days she was patched up and pumped out. So far as I could gather, what had happened was that a shaft-bearing had given way and opened up the stuffing-box, which is the point at which the shaft passes through the hull. This had allowed too much water to enter for the pumps to cope with. Many another vessel has suffered such accidents and survived to sail another day. Not so the *Enterprise*. She quietly took flight and never returned. She was not "safe." Her Orillian rival had won, and remained to ply the lake in lonely grandeur for another dozen years. That sinking marks the closing of an era. It symbolizes the passing of the little steamboats, the end of navigation on the inland lakes of Ontario.

And may I add my best compliments to the shade of that rare master, Leacock, for the successful and shameless way in which he stole for his town the very weakness of the Barrie steamer, her death in fact? It is true that he talks of outlandish places like Mariposa, Lake Wissanotti, the Lower Ossawippi and other synthetic Indian remainders, but those in the secret know well enough where that stretch of the lake is "from the big reed beds to within a mile of the town wharf:" it is suspiciously close to Orillia—the waters of the rival town are clear and cold and deep. To take a really noble ship—Leacock himself says that after you've been in Mariposa for a month or two and paddled alongside the *Mariposa Belle* in a canoe, you see no difference between her and the *Lusitania*—to take a really noble ship, and reduce her to a mere scow on a shallow little lake, after she had been breasting for decades the waves of one of Canada's minor inland seas, to advertise her last sad trip in that unmistakeable Orillian journal, the *Newspacket*, all this, I contend, as a Barrieite, was a typically Orillian piece of work.

III

On the "Pewabic" to Ombabika

I WAS just twenty, and had never been out of the conventional surroundings of my Ontario upbringing. And now, after a year at college, I found myself plunging into the wilderness, already hundreds of miles from the familiar. At the very moment of departure, I had stepped into a new world, for with my inexperience, although I had an ordinary ticket, I had got into an old colonist car. It was filled with Italian labourers on their way to the northern mines; a few hours of their noisy, gay talk showed me that there were other people in the world beside the solid, inarticulate men whom I had hitherto regarded as normal.

As the train sped westward, darkness fell, but I woke myself up at daylight, eager to catch the first glimpse of what I knew lay up ahead, Lake Superior. At last it came; a great shining in the sun, a great glitter out there to the southwest. Those were the days before Canada had been revealed to the eyes of Canadians. Since then, that northshore country as I saw it that May morning in the sun has been put down on canvas by Lawren Harris. If you don't like his pictures, you may have been through that country, but you have not seen it.

All day we skirted the lake and in the late afternoon the train drew in to my destination, Nipigon; a place of which, until a few days before, I had never heard and in

whose existence it seemed hard to believe. But soon after
arriving, I encountered some other young men who were
on the same mission as myself. We were all to serve as
"fire-rangers" for the Ontario government, patrolling the
line of railway that was being built across the north of
the Province. The other fellows turned out to be students
also. This gave me the necessary link with the known
and brought "Nipigon" down to earth.

My companions were bulging with exciting news.
They had just come in from Lake Helen, which is the
first expansion of the Nipigon River above the point at
which it crosses the railway. There they had been, they
said, "dragging." "Dragging?" Yes, dragging. A day or
two before, four Swedes, coming down from "the line"
had been caught in a storm on Lake Helen and drowned.
They had been dragging for the bodies.

"Lake Helen", "the line", "Swedes". How the cur-
tains were rolling back! Nameless strangers casually
drowned!

Our instructions were to go up to the north end of
Lake Nipigon at Ombabika Bay and there report for
duty. We began our journey at once. A little tug ran
up Lake Helen to the head of navigation. Here a narrow-
gauge railway had been put through the bush to South
Bay and from that point there was a steamer to
Ombabika. Before the tug left, provincial policemen
carefully inspected the men who were going up to "the
line" (the trans-continental railway then being built,
now the northern line of the Canadian National.) Nearly
all of these were foreigners, part of the great army of
cheap European labour that trailed across our soil in the
years before the First World War. The policemen were
watching for liquor, the worst enemy of the railway
building contractor. Women, the contractor would
tolerate—on the outskirts of the camp; he rather welcomed
them, for they kept the men contented. Liquor, however,

was taboo, for it meant drunken bouts and idleness.
Many a bottle was whisked out of hip-pockets as we
watched.

We reached the lake that night, and without incident,
though I must confess I was alarmed at what did duty
for a railway. The little engine and its narrow cars rushed
wildly through the bush, over deep chasms on the slender-
est of bridges, and up and down grades that no respectable train is called on to face. It was my first taste of
pioneer expediency.

In the morning, we embarked on the *Pewabic*. She
was a small vessel for that big lake, which at some points
has a clear sweep of fifty or sixty miles, and she was heavily
loaded, both with cargo and passengers. The new railway, for a stretch of a couple of hundred miles, east and
west, had, as its only supply base, this route from Nipigon
station on the Canadian Pacific to the head of Lake
Nipigon: the *Pewabic* and one other boat carried every
pound of flour, every stick of dynamite and every man-
jack engaged on that stretch of construction. From the
steamers' various points of call around the north end of
the lake, supplies were moved in to the "right of way"
over the canoe routes; it is perhaps not necessary to explain that the Canadian northland consists in endless
chains of lakes and rivers, between and along which for
centuries the Indian canoe routes have run. The rail-
road builders just improved them a little by building
"tote roads" over the portages. Every piece of freight,
heavy or light, every passenger, that came off the steamers,
elsewhere than at the main port of call at Ombabika Bay,
where the new road touched the lake, went up to "the
line" by canoe.

Our first stop was to be at the mouth of the Wabinosh
River, which flows into Lake Nipigon about twenty miles
north of Nipigon House, the Hudson's Bay Company's
post; up the Wabinosh lay the first of the routes in from

the lake to "the line." The morning was fine. The northern spring was just furiously bursting out. Islands lay
scattered like jewels in every direction. As we drew in
towards the river, two of them, shaped like great loaves
of bread, rose up out of the water a thousand feet. These
were the Inner and Outer Barn, solemn and impressive
specimens of the geological formation known as the
Keeweenawan, which is peculiar to the Nipigon-Thunder
Bay region.

Between Wabinosh and the next stop we cut across
wide, shallow Windigo Bay, in the centre of whose shore-
line rose a single sugar-cone, the "Haystack." Windigo
Bay, so the Indians said, was no place to be caught in at
night; the Windigoes would get you. Windigoes are
giants. It was certainly no place to be caught in, but for
a very good reason; it was wide and open, and if you
were crossing it by canoe, an onshore wind might blow
you into its inhospitable muskegs.

Lake Nipigon abounds in ancient Indian legends.
There is a splatter of islands out from Nipigon House
which were thrown into their present positions by Nan-
i-bo-zhoo, the tribal hero of the Ojibways; they are the
different parts of a moose which he cut up and threw
about in this off-hand way. I got quite a store of information about the Indians of the lake from a missionary priest
who came aboard at one of our landings. He was a
scholarly man and gentleman, a good sample of the old-
fashioned classical culture of French Canada. I had
occasionally seen Indians making baskets, but I had never
before talked to a Catholic priest; priests were not very
popular in South Simcoe. My Protestant innocence was
mildly disturbed at finding him so courteous and intelligent.

Our course led us through the island groups in the
north centre of the lake. These were even more pic-
turesque than those farther south. Red granite cliffs

alternated with the giants' causeways so common in the Keeweenawan formation. There was to come a time when I got the chance to walk up some of these great flights of stairs; block after block, each about two feet high, with a two foot tread, and regular as if they had been built, several hundred feet, to the tops of the islands which they composed. At the top would come the reward; mile after mile of island and lake, green, silver and blue, into the infinite distance. I have never seen blues anywhere so intense as around the Nipigon—except in the lower St. Lawrence where they are more intense still. Canada keeps these jewels of hers carelessly. Half the time she does not know that she possesses them. Who, I ask, has ever seen her wearing the gleaming Nipigon in her hair?

Going into Ombabika Bay, the lake gave us a taste of what it really could do if it wanted to be nasty. We rolled merrily as the waves choked into the strait between lake and bay. This was naturally the moment the cook chose to ring the dinner bell. The roll of the ship parted some of my companions from their meal but I am proud to report that I held on to mine. No shipping company has ever made any profit on its food at my expense. I have eaten down captains themselves!

The *Pewabic's* little dining saloon contained one table. One side of this was reserved for the captain, who must have his place of state, even in this backwoods inland craft. With him, the "white men" ate; afterwards the "bohunks" could go in, if they wished. I once tried to get from a simple man, his notion of a "bohunk." Were Galicians, "bohunks"? Without question, they were. Were Indians? They were not. Were Swedes? No, he didn't think so. Finns? Yes, probably. Germans? He was not quite sure. French Canadians? Certainly not. In those days when the north and west were being built, wherever a "bohunk" was, he was treated like a bohunk. The original sin of racialism goes deep.

Earlier in the day, I had been brandishing a pocket
compass which I had laid in as a piece of what I believed
to be appropriate bush equipment. In those days I did
not know how clumsy is the ordinary pocket compass of
the landsman compared with the simplicity of the
mariner's compass—which may be obtained in pocket
sizes too. The captain told me mine would be no good
to me anyway. "Too much iron around this lake," he
said, "draws my compass, right out on board here." The
Indian name of this little ship—*The Pewabic*—itself means
"iron." There may be too much iron, but it does not
come in commercial concentrations; there is one considerable deposit on the east shore, but it is not practicable
to mine it. Whether the iron "drew" the ship's compass
or not, the captain used to go up and down that lake
under conditions which would have terrified sailors used
to the safety of the open sea. I remember another trip
with him, on a rainy, pitch black night. He took her
down through that maze of islands—not a single one of
them with a light on it—without hesitation and without
misadventure. In Canada, if you are looking for sailors,
you must not confine your search to salt water.

After we had made the entrance to Ombabika Bay, we
ran over to the depot wharf and the voyage ended. Re-
porting for duty, I was promptly put into a canoe and
despatched across the bay to a portage, where, with two
or three others, I was told to camp until the main body
came along. During our wait, in the first week of June,
we had a snow storm. This tied up greenhorns like ourselves into unexpected and uncomfortable knots. It was
to take four good months of paddle, packstrap and axe
to make us over into something approaching bushmen.

I had left the "east" on Monday evening. And here I
was on Friday, camped on this portage, a hundred miles
or more from a railway. It seemed more like five years
than five days, so vastly and suddenly had my experience

of men and things widened. There is no more provincial
soul than the inhabitant of Southern Ontario, especially
of that central region whose numerous small towns gear
tightly into the largest member of their class, Toronto,
for it forms a *cul-de-sac* in Canada, unaware in any vital
way of the rest of the country and satisfied with what it
believes to be as high a civilization as can be achieved—
short of the British Isles themselves! ! ! Until that mo-
mentous journey to the head of Lake Nipigon, nothing
had occurred to make me aware of myself in relation to
that provincial society, which I had never had a look at
from the outside. I had taken it completely for granted, as
the norm of existence. But now the mould was broken.
I had joined the fraternity of the frontier, and was to take
part in that attack on the wilderness, that job of building,
that collective act of faith, which had made America
and was making Canada.

IV

The Sea of the North:

Down to the Northern Sea

WHEN THE PEOPLE of Ontario think of the sea, their minds as a rule turn to the great ports, to New York, London, Montreal. But the Province has a sea of its own, just over the height of land across its own northern region of bush and lake. The Sea of the North, *la Mer du Nord*, as the French called it in the old days, is only three hours' flight from Ontario's capital. But in the minds of most Ontario people it is less real and more distant than the Pacific.

In the summers I spent in the northern Ontario bush long ago, many a time did my thoughts turn to that far northern sea. How often, as I saw the brown waters tumbling away northward, did I long to put my canoe in to them and paddle down to their destination far below. My memory as I write is filled with the sight of that rapids which breaks out of Allanwater, a hundred miles eastward of Sioux Lookout, or of the river stretching away northward from Fort Metagami. No one at the Fort could have avoided knowing the destination of that river, for the old birch freighting canoes were still in the canoe sheds and old "Colonel" Millar, the postkeeper, who had come out through Hudson's Straits in 1870, still full of the stories of how goods in the old days were freighted up from salt water, three hundred miles below.

Perhaps only those who have faced the bush with a paddle in their hands can know the urge of the river: it will draw a man up, or it will draw him down, but draw him it will, as it drew the fur traders—inland to the centre of the continent and right through out on its other side. In all of us who used to be together in the bush in those old days, the draw of the northern rivers leading to the northern sea was discernible, but virtually none of us ever imagined it could have its way.

To this day those who have seen the northern sea, even by railway, are few and fewer still are those who have gone down to it and come again by canoes. The trip down river is long and arduous, the trip back hard indeed. It was rarely made when men used canoes: it must still be infrequent in these days of planes and outboards. Hudson's Bay, Canada's great inland sea, pressing in towards Lake Superior, cuts into the country's middle, giving it that "wasp waist" appearance so evident on the map. Yet the waist itself, though comparatively narrow from the lakes across to salt water, has remained one of the stubborn bits of Canadian geography, and even today is almost entirely wilderness. With its lakes and its rivers, its rocks and especially its muskegs, it is a difficult country. It has always proved an effective barrier between white men to the south and white men on the sea to the north. In the old days, those men were French and English. Today they are ordinary Canadians and the northern fur traders, but the gap between them remains.

Little did I ever dream in those old "bush" days of mine that the chance might come to me to make that crossing and descend the northern watershed to the sea. Old Pere Albanel had blazed the trail two centuries and a half before when he had gone from the Saguenay and Lake St. John and down by the Rupert River to head

off the English. He was two years too late for that but
his countryman, the Chevalier de Troyes, fifteen years
later, did it effectually enough, when he went up the
Ottawa, through Lakes Temiscaming and Abitibi and
down the Abitibi river, to burn the English posts. However strongly I had felt the attraction of that northern
sea when in the bush along the height of land, I had
never dreamed that the chance actually would come my
way to follow in the footsteps of the great men of old and
myself make the crossing.

That, however, is just what did happen. The chance
did come my way. One day I opened a letter and had my
breath taken away by reading that I had been selected to
take a small Canadian government party down to James
Bay and proceed up its western coast to Cape Henrietta
Maria. The object was to collect data on the possibilities
for commercial fishing. An oversize freight canoe was
provided, funds, fishnets and two men. Supplies, route,
procedure, were entirely at my discretion. It was an
opportunity fit for a king: in charge of an expedition to
the relatively far north! On my own! And not yet twenty-
five!

After the necessary departmental consultations in
Ottawa, I went to Cochrane, Ontario, the natural point
of departure. There were plenty of people there ready
to talk about routes but few who really knew anything
about them. The northern line of the Canadian National
was just then under construction: it made the journey
much easier than it had been previously, for it cut across
the rivers flowing north and saved the long trip over the
height of land. Of northward flowing rivers there is no
end: the Nottaway and the Harricanaw in Quebec; in
central Ontario, all those that unite to form the Moose:
the Abitibi, the Frederickhouse, the Metagami, the
Groundhog, the Missinabi, the Kapuskasing and many
others; further west, the Pagatchewan, the Nagogami, the

Kabinokogami, all tributaries of the Albany. The route from the railway down to Moose Factory was about two hundred miles long, and, by report, full of portages and rough water. By the Albany and its tributaries, the distance was nearly four hundred miles, but this brought me out a hundred miles further up the west coast of the Bay and the information I got about it was much the same as Radisson and Groseilliers must have received when, wandering about in the country at the head of Lake Superior in the 1650's, they, first of white men, learned of a route to "The Sea of the North": "put your canoe in Albany waters and you can float right down to the sea." I had thus good precedent, and decided for the Albany, via its tributary, the Nagogami, which flows into the Kenogami and thence into the Albany. This turned out to be far the best route, and surprisingly easy, for there were only fifteen or twenty miles of bad water, and that just below the railway line. These passed, there was nothing but smooth paddling all the way down. On this great river system, a good-sized vessel could be brought up from the sea to within a few miles of the "line"; some day this fact will get the attention it deserves.

At the Nagogami crossing, there was a group of Indians encamped: most of them were Ojibways who did not know the northern water, but there was one Cree among them who did. He was a native of the Bay and his very presence carried with it a whiff of salt air. He was well off his beat, so far inland, but his being there showed we were now in a zone of tribal contact, with inlanders to the south and coast Indians to the north. I hired the Cree to take us down through the first few dangerous rapids. He proved supremely competent. I still can see the white water tearing at the rocks in the worst of the rapids, one forming a great arc of a circle where the river turned. The Cree stood in the bow, and as a rock approached, a barely perceptible movement of his paddle would draw the bow off from it and into safety. Deceptive long smooths, oily in their stillness, with vicious, curling, destructive waves at their end, foretelling hidden rocks, would go by harmlessly, the invisible skill of the man's wrists fending us off from disaster. At top speed, through foam and broken water, we tore down, but my guide brought the great canoe through as easily as a boy runs his sleigh down a hill. Thanks to him, we were through the rapids and had made camp, all in a few hours from 'the line', with nothing but smooth water between us and our destination.

It is easy to put it that way, but only those who have had the experience can know what a sense of physical and spiritual excitement comes to one who turns his face away from men towards the unknown. In his small way he is doing what the great explorers have done before him, and his elation recaptures theirs. The last houses disappear, the unbroken forest comes down to the water's edge, the little party is alone in the vastness, with only a question mark ahead of it. It is like seeing the land fade out on the horizon, with the trackless ocean ahead.

A day brought us to Mamawemattawa, "the great confluence"; here several brimming rivers join together into the Kenogami, "the long river", a big stream in its own right. A day or two down it, and then, that which will always remain an experience for me, no matter how often it is repeated, wider waters appear ahead, as if through some gigantic window, and suddenly the river *pops* into a greater than itself: a junction has been effected. In this case it was the Albany itself which appeared in the show-window; and now with a few strokes, we were out on it, out on the broad waters of this great and beautiful river, this river which is yet more remote to most Canadians (who of all people fail in appreciative knowledge of Canada) than Rhine or Nile. The Albany may be over-shadowed by the mighty Nelson on the north and the still mightier St. Lawrence on the south, but there I was on it, on the waters which Radisson and Groseilliers would have given so much to dip their paddles in. From their day to mine, the people who had descended this river to the sea were in all probability fewer in number than those who travel from Toronto to Montreal in the course of a single week.

Mile after mile we travelled on, making good speed with the current behind us. The great river was unimpeded by rapids and so broad and straight that sometimes a horizon appeared ahead. I knew what lay at the end of our road but I could not imagine it.

For several days we had this vast northern country to ourselves, and did not encounter a living soul, or the sign of one. Then we met people again: a big party of Indians taking in the annual supplies to Fort Good Hope. They were not using canoes but were tracking up a York boat which is like an overgrown river punt, but pointed at both ends. The banks of the Albany are wide and smooth, and it is therefore easy to walk along, a dozen or fifteen men on the tracking line, towing the boat. The supply brigade and the York boat spoke of another world, far out of the orbit of the railway, a world that had already been going on like this long generations before, when Frenchman and Nor'Wester were paddling up through the lakes to the *pays d'en haut.*

On the tenth day, rounding a bend, I noticed that the shores were wet and muddy: there was a space between the water and the bank where nothing grew. This could mean only one thing. Typical Ontarian that I was, I had never seen the sea. I had always assumed that some day I would see it when I made the conventional Ontario pilgrimage to England, but at that moment I did not know a tide mark when I saw it. Yet in my unorthodox approach to the sea, sneaking up on it from the rear in this way, I was in a good tradition. Thompson and Fraser had gone down the Columbia and the Fraser in that way, and the greatest of them all, Mackenzie, had come upon the Arctic and the Pacific, too, "by land, from Canada." But they were all outlanders, to whom the sea had no doubt long been familiar. There had been few native born Canadians in that long line: Louis Joliet, first to descend the Mississippi, the great La Verendrye and others of lesser note. I did not compare myself to these giants, for that would have been nonsense, but I felt that I was treading in their footsteps.

Another hour's paddling brought into view some distant objects that looked like houses. One learns to distrust such impressions in the bush. But a little more paddling, and they were houses. Our canoe drew abreast of the first of them. A man came down to meet us. He spoke in a slightly foreign accent and proved to be the deputy post-manager of Revillon Frères, who in those years were in strong competition throughout the north with the Hudson's Bay Company. Almost his first words were "Have you any news?" This sounded strange, until it dawned on me that he had been cut off from the outside world for months: there were no radios in those days. After a chat, we paddled on to the Hudson's Bay post which gives its name to the little settlement, Fort Albany. It was hard to realize that here, on this river bank, life at that moment was going on much as it had been doing long before English Canada had come into existence and that on this precise spot, where now English and French were peaceful rivals, two centuries and a half before they had waged bloody battles with each other, and for the furs which in those days as today, came down the great river whose descent I had just made. It was curious to reflect that I had had to come all this distance through the bush to obtain that sense of history which my native habitat could not supply.

When we reached the Hudson's Bay post, I was greeted by the factor in words which were only a variant of those of the first man: "How's everything down in Canada?" was what the factor said. So I was no longer in Canada? Not in the opinion of the dwellers at the mouth of the Albany, apparently: they lived in a separate world, whose traditions did not lead south through the bush but out across the ocean, to the ports whence for nine generations had come their supplies and their men.

I walked up a little rise past the post. The river was wide and impressive. The high ground fell away in flats. The moment was come: the moment dreamed about around inland campfires. I had emerged on "the other side." For out there beyond the flats, beyond the stretch of the river, I saw a thin grey line where sky and water met: I was looking out over the horizon, out over "The Sea of the North."

V

The Sea of the North:
From Albany to Attawapiskat

HAVING REACHED the "Sea of the North," I had to plan
my summer's work. My instructions were to proceed up
the coast, collecting information on the prospects for commercial fishing and in whatever way seemed practicable.
Everybody at Albany stood ready to do what they could
for me, though I was amused at the Scottish caution of
the Hudson's Bay Factor, Mr. Gillies. Apparently he at
first thought I might be an Ontario game warden and was
careful to inform me that he had no furs about: he felt
relieved, he said, when he heard of my arrival, to recol-
lect that he had just sent them all over to the central
depot, on Charlton Island, which, he dropped in in-
cidentally, was in Quebec province. I was left to add for
myself "and therefore out of my reach." When he found
that I was an emissary of the harmless government at
Ottawa, come on an innocent quest for mere information,
he lowered his guard. After I got well acquainted with
him, which in a spot like Albany naturally did not take
long, although he continued cautious about giving out
information that the Company might conceivably
(though with difficulty) regard as confidential, he proved
helpful and hospitable, a man of character.

I became close friends with the Anglican missionary, the Rev. Mr. Griffin. He gave me free access to all the mission records, going back to the times of the good Bishop Horden in the 1860's. In their pages could be seen break-up and freeze-up, seasons of scarcity and seasons of plenty, rejoicings over Indians saved and grief over those who would not forsake their heathen ways. One entry recorded a trip out to Canada by way of the Albany, the Ogoki and the Nipigon to Lake Superior. The missionary of the time remarked, after passing through Lake Nipigon, on how pleasant and smiling a region it was and how easy life seemed there for the Indians compared with the stern James Bay: there are degrees of "north."

Life at Albany was unavoidably isolated but neither boorish nor boring. The white community was small but its members were all of good calibre. It consisted of M. Pecodie, the assistant post-keeper for Revillon Frères, his wife, Mr. and Mrs. Griffin, Mr. Gillies, his wife and married daughter and the Catholic priests and nuns. The Pecodies were two highly intelligent people and Mme. Pecodie one of the best cooks who ever invited me to a meal: the dinner she served was as elegant as if we had been in Paris. The Griffins were good, kind people but I am afraid that the existence, in this remote outpost, of the same rigid wall between Protestant and Catholic as characterized my native county of Simcoe had to be put down in some measure to the North of Ireland origin of my friend Griffin. Talking about one of his Indians who had been seriously ill, and had been taken to the little hospital kept by the nuns, he said to me one day: "I stood it as long as I could, thinking of him lying there among crucifixes and with the priests around him, and then I walked right in to see him: I just went right into the midst of them." The heavens didn't seem to fall either.

As a matter of fact, the Canadian priests I met in the north—all of them Oblates from Ottawa—seemed to me

a very decent lot, men of fine manners and human feeling, and well-trained for their work. Their whole cultural
pattern, of course, was very different from that of my
missionary friend and from my own, and I can understand some of his instinctive feelings of hostility. Better
education gave them a considerable advantage over the
Anglican missionaries: this enabled them to learn the
difficult Cree language more easily than did the Anglicans,
to whom it always remained a stumbling block. But to
say this is not to disparage any of the English-speaking
missionaries I met, especially my friend Griffin and his
wife, who could not have been better or more sincere
people.

Mr. Gillies procured me a third man, a half-breed who
knew all the camp-spots: he could pick out a little bluff
or the mouth of a creek miles off shore when all I could
see would be the occasional thin blue whisp in the distance. When Moses fired at a duck and missed, he always
called out cheerfully "Very nigh," but when anyone else
fired and missed, he would roar half derisively "No good!"

I got my training in west coast canoeing under Moses.
James Bay represents the extension under water, and at
the slightest possible angle, of the flat table land of Northern Ontario and Quebec. As a consequence, its banks are
low and flat and the water for several miles off shore is
extremely shallow. The tide rises vertically about twelve
feet. Since the slope is so slight, the horizontal distance
represented by twelve feet of a rise is enormous. There
are several miles between the edge of the sea at high water
and its edge at low. Above the tidemark the shore takes
another two or three miles to make up its mind whether
it is really going to become dry land or not: this is a belt
of grass and bullrush intersected by innumerable tidal
creeks. Then low willow shrubs begin, and a mile or two
further on, the tree line, which quickly deepens into the
dark spruce forest of the north. An exceptionally high

tide will cover all this foreshore and at low water the sea practically disappears below horizon. The intervening miles of tidemark consist of soft mud with the occasional hard ridge on which a man can stand without sinking up to his knees. The shore, such as it is, is just a grassy bank, though here and there there are pebble beaches scraped up by wave and ice. The marshes are alive with the thickest clouds of the largest mosquitoes known to man. The only compensation for all this—and it is a considerable one—is that these interminable rushes and reeds provide the best wildfowl shooting on the continent.

To paddle along this shore, the Indians have developed methods which are as tedious as they are prudent. The day we left Albany, we paddled about three hours and then about three in the afternoon. Moses brought the canoe up on the shore. He indicated we were to camp for the night. I was rather annoyed, as, at that rate of travel, it seemed to me we would never get anywhere. However, within an hour or two, no water was to be seen, so it was evident that the alternative would have been to go on out beyond the tidemark until the tide came again at about two in the morning. Very sensibly, no Indian will do this. When the tide answers, it is possible to paddle for a few hours in the morning, "sit on the mud" from, say, ten to three, and then paddle for a couple of hours after the afternoon high water. If the afternoon paddling period is stretched out too long, there is danger of having to pass the night "sitting on the mud" or paddling in the dark: weather changes are too sudden to risk that. I remember once making in to the shore on an ebb tide, and finding the water draining out from under us with lightning speed; we had to step out into the mud, wading up to our thighs, and pull the canoe right through it before we got up to the "beach."

I made for the Kapiskau, the first large river north of the Albany. This stream has a narrow entrance but opens up into a good safe harbour. The Cree word means "the closed-up place," "the narrows." The equivalent word to *Kapiskau* (phonetically *Kaybesko*) among the Indians of the St. Lawrence would be *Kaybeko*. This is the word that Champlain heard when he came through the narrows at the Island of Orleans into the first safe harbour up from the sea. Antiquarians have for generations wrangled over the meaning of the name of Canada's historic city but a little knowledge of Cree and Objibway would have saved a great deal of ink. Kaybeko, or Quebec (pronounced, it is to be remembered, *Kaybeck* in French) is just "the closed-up place," "the narrows."

We camped at the mouth of the Kapiskau. That night the moon was gloriously bright and large over the grassy lands. It sparkled on river and on the distant sea; it lit up the dim line of the forest. Not a sound disturbed the still, keen northern night. It was a night, which, under the spell of the flooding moonlight, united man with all nature, a marvellous night. More marvellous still, there were no mosquitoes. But in the morning, there were other visitors, two of them: two husky dogs sitting patiently outside the tent, waiting for us to wake up. They had been left by their owners to shift for themselves during the summer. There was no human being within fifty miles, but the dogs, living on the country, were fat as butter. What is more, they were the only huskies I have ever encountered who were not shameless thieves. And were they glad to see us! And did they voice their grief when we paddled off! True gentlemen, both.

After the Kapiskau comes the Attawapiskat, a large river reaching back several hundred miles into the flat clay lands of the Ontario district of Patricia. In those days, Revillon Frères had a permanent post there, but the Hudson's Bay Company did not. There was also a Catholic mission with a resident priest. Attached to the post were three men, two from Quebec and one, Tom Bates, born on the Bay. The four white men at Attawapiskat were unique up there in that they were all Canadians. I did not meet a single other English Canadian during my sojourn on James Bay and only three French Canadians, apart from the priests. Everyone else had been born abroad. There were a few whites, of whom Tom Bates was one, who had been born on the Bay and had never been off it. Technically, I suppose, they were Canadians.

Like many of the whites up there, Tom Bates was married to a squaw. Should he ever see these lines, I hope he will forgive me but the story told about him and his lady does deserve rescue from oblivion, for few men can put up such a valiant struggle against matrimony as did Tom. Tom left Moose Factory and struck north to avoid the parson. But the parson was a determined man. He set out in pursuit. Tom moved on, past Albany, past the Kapiskau, with the parson still in pursuit. Tom came to Attawapiskat: the parson followed. There remained the uninhabited north: Tom struck bravely out. So did the parson. Finally on the banks of some remote creek he ran down his man, after full four hundred miles of chase, bundled him into his canoe, brought him back and demanded that he "marry the girl." Tom did.

The postmaster at Attawapiskat, whom I shall call Delarue, was minus the toes on his right foot. Two winters before, he had begun to walk home from Agumski Island, which lies twenty miles out to sea. Darkness overtook him before he got to the post and he wandered into the tidemark, where he got wet and froze his feet. They took him to the hospital at Albany but there were neither nurses nor doctors among the nuns there. Gangrene set in. Everyone was afraid to try to amputate his toes, but at last, knowing that if they were not taken off, he would

die anyway, he set about the job himself, and without
antiseptics or surgical knowledge, cut his own toes off,
saving his life.

My French friends at Attawapiskat were inveterate
card players. The game was "Five Hundred." My
presence afforded them a convenient fourth. On Sunday
evenings we would begin three-handed, waiting for Father
Beaudry to finish his service. The Father always seemed
to win. "You never can beat de fader," Delarue would
exclaim, "he have de devil's own luck, de fader." Delarue's
assistant was one Trudeau, from Three Rivers. He was a
simple, good-hearted, unlettered man. I remember his
excusing himself one evening, when both the others happened to be away somewhere. We were chatting and he
remarked quite simply: "I'll have to go now. There's an
Indian woman who's going to have a child, and I'll have to
go over and look after her." In the north, the white man
is omniscient, and the unlettered fur-trader must and does
rise to the occasion.

Attawapiskat was an outpost, far in the bush,
genuinely "backwoods" as compared with Albany. But
I cannot say I found life dull there: I worked my nets
every day and at night. I had good company. The wilderness calls out whatever there is in a man: he does not go
to pieces or become a clod merely because there is no
movie to go to. And often in simple men, there is a great
deal to call out.

VI

The Sea of the North:
"Farthest North"

THE ATTAWAPISKAT RIVER comes in about half way up
the west coast of James Bay. We had set our nets at its
southern mouth, the Lowashi, and at various points in its
main channel. The catch was not impressive: the fish
had not yet begun to come in from the sea. Now it was
necessary to go on further north and find out if they were
beginning to come in there earlier than toward the south.
A good many rivers entered the northern, or upper, half
of the west coast but none of them was overly important,
so when I found out that the big schooner *Hilda P.* was
to go north without making intermediate stops at any of
them, I decided to go in her. I could do the intervening
rivers on the way down.

The *Hilda P.* belonged to Revillon Frères and was to
carry supplies to their outpost on the Opinegau, the last
stream of any consequence before Cape Henrietta Maria.
The Hudson's Bay Company—"the old Company"—had
outposts only at the Kapiskau and Attawapiskat, none
further north. An "outpost" was simply a storehouse,
with a man put in charge for the period the Indians were
outfitting prior to departing for their winter hunting
grounds. As its more numerous posts and outposts sug-

35

gested, it seemed to me that the French company had
managed to secure the major share of the business along
the coast. This meant that most of the Indians north of
Albany were "French company Indians." This rivalry
between the two companies divided the Indians into two
quite distinct camps, for they obviously had to take their
furs back to the company which had advanced them their
autumn supplies. If an Indian ever could have got "out
of the red" and on a cash basis, he would have been able
to buy his supplies wherever he pleased, but for some
reason or other, no matter how good his winter's catch,
he always wound up in debt to the outfitting company.
Under these circumstances, woe betide the Indian who
attempted to "put it over" the supplying company by
taking his furs to the other one. He could do that just
once, then the chains were rivetted on him. Every Indian
was thus either a "Company Indian" or a "French Company Indian."

As far as I could observe the division was accentuated
by religion. Roman Catholic Indians gravitated to Revillon Frères (this was natural in view of the language
affinities between traders and priests), Protestant Indians
were traditional "Company Indians." Most of the half-
breeds were intermarried on the English side: they were
bilingual and Protestants. The half-breed usually did
not go out to the winter hunting grounds, but earned his
living in second rank company employment. His
economic status was higher than that of the Indian: he
lived in a cabin and worked for wages, whereas the essence
of the trapper relationship was that the trapper worked
for bare subsistence in terms of goods.

The *Hilda P.* was an able ship, built on the Bay out
of timber grown on its shores. She was quite equal to
going out to sea: in fact, she probably was larger than
many of the vessels by which the Bay had originally been

explored. But she, too, had to conform to local custom
and "sit on the mud" at low tide. This made our voyage
as slow as working north by canoe.

We dropped down to the river mouth, where we waited for the tide. Here without knowing it, I committed a
serious offence: I stripped off, turned over the side and
took a swim. Almost immediately, the wind turned into
the north and kept us from getting out of the river. I
did not know it at the time but I discovered later on,
while we continued to be plagued with head winds, that
this is always what happens when a man bares his body
before other men.

Somehow or other the Indian gods must have been
appeased, for we got a fair wind at last, and ran on up
through the strait that separates Agumski Island from
the mainland. Towards evening the ship bumped and
stuck. It was not a shipwreck but merely marked the end
of the day's work: sail was furled and we settled down
comfortably on the mud. In the morning the tide was in,
the wind was howling from the north and in sea parlance,
we were "rolling our guts out." This made it difficult
to perform certain necessary personal tasks which involved
sitting far out over the gunwale and hanging on by a
shroud: at one moment you were suspended in space
twenty feet above the water, and at the next, virtually in it.

The Indian sailors decided we would have to seek
shelter, so we ran back to where a low ridge in the bottom
gave a certain protection, and there we lay while once
more the tide left us and the grey mud appeared. It was
evident that we were there for at least another twenty-four
hours, as the tide would not make again until evening,
and there would certainly be no sailing after dark. My
half-breed guide, Moses Wesley, requested permission
to go hunting: he thought he might find a caribou. "But
you have no rifle, Moses," I said. He timidly suggested
that he might perhaps borrow mine. I let him have it,

and he and an Indian went off together, walking knee-
deep in mud for a couple of miles until they got to shore,
then across the grass and willow prairie into the bush.
They were away all day, and got back to the schooner
just before the night tide began to make. They had not
found any caribou. That was the first and last time I
have ever seen hunters walk off a ship lying at anchor into
the forest.

Next day the Indian gods smiled on us with a fair
wind from the south, and we set sail again. This time
the sun sparkled, the sea took on deep hues of blue and
came alive with hundreds of white whales: these fellows
were rolling their white backs everywhere, like the rims
of great moons just showing out of the water. Seals, too,
were numerous. You have to be quick to get a seal with
a rifle. It is not too difficult to hit him, but he is heavy
and unless you can get right up to him at once (in canoe
or kayak), he will sink. That day will always stand out
for me: blue sea, blue sky, white whales, laughing, joking
Indians, the good ship driving on under two jibs, fore
and mainsail, making good speed and rolling out the
crushed foam from her bows with the music that only
a sailing ship's bows can make. There was just one dis-
cordant note. Toward afternoon, far out to sea, a white
line appeared. As we came closer to it, we saw what it
was: a long line of ice, mile after mile of it, sweeping
north, to be lost in the immensity of Hudson's Bay—the
last spring icefield moving out. It was July 23.

One good wind took us up to the Opinegau, a little
muddy river just large enough to get the *Hilda P.* into
at high water. The big schooner was run up on the
muddy fore shore. As the tide went out, she lay high
and dry, and the supplies could be unloaded from her
without need of any wharf. From the landing they were
"toted" up stream three or four miles and put in the
winter post.

At the Opinegau, I had my introduction to yellow-legs hunting. The Greater Yellow-legs is a marsh bird standing on stilts six or eight inches high: the Lesser Yellow-legs is a little smaller and has no stilts. Both species frequent the James Bay marshes in huge numbers. They get very wary in the fall but, during the summer, they are easy to shoot: in fact, as they keep close together, one fortunate shot will sometimes kill three or four. We ate them boiled and we ate them fried and we ate them roasted, and they were equally good every way. Two of them made just an ample meal. All day long, the marshes were noisy with the guns of the Indians, who in mid-summer find in the "Shee-shay-shoo" (a word which imitates the notes of these birds) one of their chief sources of food.

I left the *Hilda P.* on the mud of the Opinegau and turned my canoe once more to the north. This was not accomplished without difficulty, for the men I had were not of the sort to greet the unknown with a cheer. Moses, the half-breed, was sturdy, but tended to be overcautious, and like all of Indian blood, anxious to get back to his family. The other two, who had been selected for me before we left Cochrane, were not fortunate choices. They were a father and son from Lake Temiskaming, Robert and Joe King. Robert, who had some Indian blood, had been born at Moose Factory some sixty-five years before. He spoke Cree naturally, though Moses used to laugh at him "because he sounded funny," which suggested that in the half-century since he had left the Bay, the language had changed a good deal. His language and his boyhood associations with the Bay did not compensate for his age. Years before, he had gone inland and married a French half-breed wife. His son Joe, who surely could hardly have been a more representative frontier mixture—part English, part French, Cree and Ojibway—whether because of this or simply because he was Joe, was a rather sour irresponsible. Neither father nor son wanted to go out on the Cape because they had heard stories of bad weather and polar bears. Looking back, I can see that part of the trouble with them lay in my own inadequate devices of leadership. The product of our equalitarian Canadian society, I did not understand that the leader, in order to maintain allegiance, confidence and prestige, must keep himself remote and that he must not debate but command. Like other young Canadians (with the exception of those who have an instinctive grasp of such things, who must be few), I found it natural to be "chummy" and to discuss. That will not do. Democracy as we understand it is a splendid concept, but the English with their rigid class training in their public schools, know far more about the art of leadership than our democracy can ever teach us.

However, I got the party moving and we set out. Our destination was the Cape—Cape Henrietta Maria, where James and Hudson's Bay join. In 1632, Captain James, the discoverer of the Bay that bears his name, called the Cape after the French wife of Charles I. It is one of the few spots in modern Canada to bear a name coming down from the Stuart period. There was really no more difficulty in pushing on from the Opinegau than there had been in working our way up from Albany, but perhaps the natives are wise in their caution: the North can turn on the traveller with astonishing speed, and when it shows its teeth, it means business.

We made our camp on one of the small streams of the Cape Region. It would have been tempting to go on further, round the corner, but that would have been exceeding my instructions, and, anyway, there was the important engagement lying ahead of me that fall to which I shall refer in a later sketch and which at the time, I thought would take me, not only back to "Canada" but across the ocean. I remember taking a picture of our big canoe lying there on the mud, and this I labelled, half-seriously, "Farthest North." Next day, our return began. The weather had been good, and the gentle southerly breeze almost persuaded us that we were in an easy country. Then, suddenly, the wind, swooping down from Hudson Bay, swung into the north and instantly the temperature dropped. Frost, perhaps snow, was near. The small Sea of the North could be severe enough, but when the great Sea of the North spoke, it spoke imperatively. "Go home, Southron," it said.

Today, a few hours' flying would cover as much ground as I covered that summer in weeks of paddling and sailing. It seems rather unfair, somehow. Man's machines eat up distance: perhaps they are eating up the earth, too.

VII

The Sea of the North:
Southward from the Cape

FROM THE CAPE, I had some three hundred miles to cover
to Albany: thence to Moose Factory another hundred,
and from Moose Factory to "the line," which was the
route I intended to take, about another two hundred,
say about six hundred in all. This I expected to do by
canoe. The most important season for my inquiries was
now at hand, late August and September, when the fish,
which have spent the summer out at sea, begin to come
in on the coast, preparatory to spawning. Yet I had to
be back before freeze-up, which in those northern waters
could conceivably come in October, and there was also
a private reason requiring my return before the end of
September: before I left in the spring, I had been in
receipt of an appointment at the Colonial Institute, Hamburg, Germany. There I was to spend two years, lectur-
ing on Canadian subjects and working towards a higher
degree. That appointment was never to be taken up:
other events would have made it awkward to keep.

Each day, as we worked our few miles further down,
we set nets either on the open coast or at the mouths of
streams: few fish were taken at first, but the number
slowly increased. The principal species were whitefish

and trout, with pickerel and pike in the river mouths. The trout was the ordinary brook or speckled trout (*salvelinus fontinalis*) of regions farther south, but the average angler would hardly be prepared for these northern fellows, for they went up to seven and eight pounds in weight. I have never tasted better fish than the northern "sea-run" speckled trout: his size, and the cold, salt water turn him, so to speak, into the very personification of fish desirability.

As I wished to explore the possibilities of the great island lying off the west coast—Agumski—when I got back to Attawapiskat, I hired one of the small post schooners and crossed over the twenty mile strait. Agumski was rather pleasant after the mainland, being wooded down to the shores and with some nice, clean beaches. As we approached the island, we saw a couple of Indian tepees. These were surrounded with what seemed a thick mist, confined to the few feet of their immediate vicinity. This extremely local fog seemed strange, for it was a bright day. Going ashore, I found the reason for it. Indian encampments, with their refuse, their dogs and their strong smelling humans, are never exactly bowers of roses. In this case, it was the odour which gave rise to the "mist," which proved to be nothing less than a thick cloud of bull-dogs! But flying bull-dogs! Each bull-dog was about three-quarters of an inch in length and armed with a pair of jaws that drew blood when they struck. The Crees call these devils "mikissik", or "eagles," and they are well-named in either language. Further south, where they are never as numerous, they are called horse-flies, or moose-flies. How the Indian families at the landing could have endured them, I do not know. Fortunately they are not quite as bloodthirsty as mosquitoes, or life around the coast would be impossible.

I remember one day glancing over the stern of the *Hilda P.* as we lay in the Opinegau. The sun was shining on it, and every square inch of that space, about twenty feet by twenty, was covered with "bull-dogs." I found a little satisfaction in taking a broom and swatting them, each blow killing hundreds. It was purposeless slaughter, I suppose, just sheer revenge, for as they say in the north, "kill one and a dozen will come to his funeral."

At the Attawapiskat, I encountered huskies who formed the strongest possible contrast to my friends at the Kapiskau: they were the most arrant thieves one could imagine. Nothing was safe from them. I remember, after one hard day, I had a very nice fish supper prepared: it was put out on a box in my tent, in the door of which I was sitting. I heard a little noise and turned round just in time to see my supper and a husky disappearing under the back of the tent. I weighted down the sides of the tent all round to keep them out, but that night every time I dozed off, I would wake with a start to find that one or more of them had forced his way in, and was beginning to rip open some package of food. At last I sat up with a paddle in my hand, and every time I saw a snout, I took a crack at it. After I had hit a sufficient number, I got some sleep.

My canoemen from the Attawapiskat southward were John Panayshees and Jimmie Kenozha Peter—John Bird and Jimmie Long Peter to you, reader. They were splendid fellows, who had been detailed to accompany me by my friend Father Beaudry, but there were two difficulties: they could speak no English and they insisted on bringing their families along. We solved this latter difficulty by keeping the two establishments entirely separate. The families, consisting of the two squaws and several children, had their own canoe, and made their own camp. The language difficulty was not so easily met. Before I left Attawapiskat, I had inquired the Cree equivalent for what I thought might be a key phrase: "What is the name of that?" It was, as I remember, "anayzinikasit." This open sesame worked wonders, and I soon acquired a small vocabulary in Cree, enough for our simple purposes of net-setting and camp-making.

These limits were exceeded one day, when John came to me and made noises that sounded like "awkwozisa mona monoshin." I knew that "mona monoshin" meant "no good," but what was awkwozisa?" He pointed it out: it was his baby girl (I can see now that "awkwozisa" is simply "little squaw," our word "squaw" being the word "awkwo," or "awkwaw," with an inserted "s"). His baby girl was no good: it was, to wit, ill. He wanted to go back to Attawapiskat. That would have left me in a hole indeed, stuck on that desolate coast in the late summer with no canoeman (for Jimmie would have probably wished to go along, too). I retired to my tent and meditated. John's oldest boy came in. I happened to have a bright new pencil in my hand: "Mashaw-winaygan atisk?" he shyly asked. I knew what that meant: could he have the pencil, the "writing stick?" I lost no time giving it to him. Then, putting on a bold face, I took some aspirin, marched over to John's tent, dissolved a tablet in water, and indicated that the baby was to be given some every two hours. I thought two hours would do as well as any other interval. What was wrong with the child, I never found out, but my bedside manner must have been good, for I heard no more of turning back.

At the Kapiskau, the scene had entirely changed from the loneliness of our first visit. The space around the little outpost buildings was covered with tents and tepees. As they noticed us coming up the river, everyone crowded to the banks: this unusual party of ours was one of the sights of a lifetime, to be gazed at with relatively the same intensity as that which greeted Jacques Cartier. While we were still well out from the landing, a long-range conversation began, the parties on shore shouting to the parties in the canoe at the tops of their voices. Coming or going, this seemed to be the custom of the country.

That evening, I saw a new form of sport. Someone had produced a football, and every man in the camp who could run joined in the game: it was not football according to any rules I had encountered. There were no sides, no goals, no limit to the number of the players: everybody just ran after the ball and kicked it hard.

A still more novel sport was August duck-hunting. August is the month when the ducks moult and are unable to fly. They hide in the long grass of the coastal marshes, where they beat down intricate runways. The idea is to chase them through the grass and hit them with a club—if you can: they are quick as lightning and all you see of them is a brown shadow scuttling away. Hunting ducks with a club may sound like a queer form of sport, but the ducks certainly have a fighting chance. I must admit I was a bit chagrined, not at the hunting, but at what happened to the ducks. First thing I knew, the Indians had them all cut up and into a pot, along with a pound or two of lard. Duck soup may be all right, but I can't take it with Indian quantities of grease.

By this time, I had been away from the "outside" for over three months and had had no word at all as to what was going on, not even any personal mail. I can't say that this bothered me: the outside world could wait. I was evidently beginning to share, temporarily, at least, the attitude of these northern people, who had their own little world, one which provided just as much interest for them as the big world does for others. In it there were adequate amounts of the same commodities as are in demand everywhere else, and upon which nine tenths of mankind normally live: absorption in the daily round, gossip, scandal, family relationships, love-making quarrelling—it is mostly a matter of scale. In one big point the northern world had the best of it—it needed no policemen. Of course the Hudson's Bay factors had traditional prestige, and they and Revillons between them had St. Peter's power of the keys—they could give or withhold supplies—so that the Indians really were to that extent under law. They had their own traditional inhibitions, too: property, for example, was absolutely safe. During the months I formed a part of it, the northern world did not need policeman or judge, for there were no offences, public or private, that I heard of.

Lapses, naturally, could occur. There was an Indian woman at one of the posts who was reputed to have killed and eaten her children out in the bush one winter. No wonder, perhaps, given the pressure of hunger and the terror the lonely forest can inspire.

About the middle of September, we had worked down to the delta of the Albany again. This time I was entering a seaport in the orthodox way, from the sea. I have always felt that sneaking up on the sea from the rear, so to speak, as I had done, and in one of its less obvious regions, had been rather unfair to it. Yet it is the way our Indians must have come upon the eastern sea, so I had been in an old tradition. As we came into Albany, we paddled up the Back Channel, across the Fishing Gut and thence to the post. So quickly does the mind adapt itself and so eagerly does it seek to find the familiar for itself that a return to this lonely northern outpost seemed like getting home.

Albany was one of the important places on the Bay— not as imposing as Moose or York, but definitely an "urban centre." As we paddled up the river, first came the Roman Catholic mission with its church, hospital and living quarters, then the Hudson's Bay post, after that a collection of cabins where the half-breeds lived, then a space of Indian tepees, more cabins, the Anglican church and school-house, the residence of my missionary friends, the Reverend Mr. Griffin and his wife, and last of all, on the edge of the bush, the most recent addition, the buildings of Revillon Frères. The little community stretched along the river bank for nearly a mile.

Here were lighted houses, tables with china dishes, even books. Here was talk, here friends. Yet there were the huskies, there the little Indian boys engaged in their unending bow-and-arrow pursuit of the squirrel, there the forest. A strange mixture: the tail-end of the primitive, the vanguard of civilization.

And there was I: still with three hundred miles of sea and wilderness between me and the railway, and with infinitely greater distances between me and the appointment I was innocently expecting to take up in Germany.

VIII

The Sea of the North:
From Albany to Stratton Island

THE *Emilia* was certainly not built for beauty. She had
a high fo'c'stle and a little pimple set well astern that
did duty for a bridge and "officers' quarters." In it were
four bunks, two on either side of the table. In most ships,
the men who occupied them would hardly have bunked
in together as "officers" for they were the skipper, the
chief (and only) engineer, the fireman and the cook-
steward. The bond between them was not status, but
skin colour: they were whites. The mate, an Indian,
despite his rank, bunked down in the fo'c'stle with the
crew, who were Indians too.

But the *Emilia,* beauty or not, came in handy. Having
arrived at Albany from the north, my problem was how
to get over to Moose Factory. If I went along the coast,
it meant hiring a crew of Indians and going back to the
tiresome business of skirting the shore by canoe. Alter-
natively I could hire a schooner and go straight across,
but it was getting a bit late for this, I was advised, being
already September. The arrival of the *Emilia* solved my
difficulties: I could go in her. After discharging at Albany, she was going back to Stratton Island, and thence
to Moose Factory to lay up for the winter. Both companies at that time sent up their yearly supplies in big

49

ships from Montreal: the Hudson's Bay vessel, the
Nascopie, unloaded at Charlton Island, that of Revillon
Frères at Stratton Island. From these points, the posts
round the Bay were supplied by the smaller ships, the
Innenew and the *Emilia.*

I said good-bye to my friends the Griffins, with whom
I had been staying while at Albany: it had been pleasant
to sleep in a bed again after some months on the ground,
and pleasant to talk over with the missionary the problems of his work: of these much could be said. But space
does not permit, and I must get aboard.

No provision seemed to have been made for my
accommodation on board and I began to wonder where
I would sleep: I did not relish the deck. The skipper said
to me, rather apologetically, "I guess you could sleep in
the hold: it'll only be for a night or two." I went and
took a look into the hold. "Seems quite a long way down
there," I called back. "Oh, I'll get one of the boys to
fetch a ladder, and you'll be all right." So the ladder was
lowered and I climbed down it. Climbing down a rope
ladder not made fast at the bottom has its own exciting
qualities: sometimes you find your feet out level with
your head.

My retreat was some twenty feet below the deck. The
hold was empty, except for spare coal. I laid my blankets
on a few boards at the edge of the coal and under the
break of the deck. The hatchway was partly covered with
a tarpaulin, but if it should rain, there was a good chance
of getting a barrel or two of water out of this, so I kept
out of range, and near the coal. At least I had space and
privacy, and I was comfortable enough.

The skipper was a Dane, an ordinary seaman who had
been washed up from a wreck a few years before, had remained and married, "country style." He had had no in-
struction in navigation but was a good seaman, and
although he had no "ticket," the company had had con-

fidence enough in him to give him this command. He was a good sample of uncut diamond. The "chief" was a short barrel-shaped man from Newfoundland. The other two in "the officers' quarters" were also from Newfoundland. They were all good fellows and, although on this small ship they were always under each others' feet, they lived harmoniously together.

We dropped down the river and fetched up just inside the bar across the river mouth. Owing to the very gradual slope of the land in that part of James Bay, although we were inside the bar, we were so far out that we could hardly see the land, except for the mud banks which appeared beyond the river channel at low tide. The skipper did not deem it advisable to try to cross the bar that night as we were in the neap tides and there probably was not water enough. He thought that by the next tide or so, we would be able to get over.

It did not turn out that way. By morning, a high wind was blowing from the southwest. This forced the water out of shallow James Bay, northward to Hudson's Bay and consequently decreased the height of the tide. So we had to wait another day for the height of high water to increase. I should perhaps explain that at neap tides, when sun and moon draw in opposite directions, high water is not so high as at "spring" tides, when sun and moon pull together, that is, at new or full moon. We were now just a day or two on the way from neaps to springs, and there should be a few more inches of water on the bar each tide.

But another morning saw the southwester blowing stronger than ever, and no visible increase in the height of high water. I have often noticed these late September southwest winds elsewhere in Canada. Nearly every fall they blow across the Ottawa valley, bringing back warm misty weather after the first forecasts of autumn have

come, giving to water and land a curious combination of
clarity and obscurity seldom seen at other times. They
come to the Lake of the Woods after an August that can
be chill and bleak, lighting up birches and poplars, holding
out encouraging hands to a summer that seems to have
been fighting a losing battle. Arthur Lismer's *September
Gale* catches the atmospheric effects of these winds. By
some trick of light, they seem to blow up the opposite
shore line, as if they were actually moving it closer: it is
this aspect of light that Lismer's picture registers. Here
was the warm Georgian Bay gale that he depicts sweeping
across us as we lay in the mouth of the Albany, preventing
us from getting out to sea.

Day after day it blew, until one wondered whether it
was not going to blow the Bay dry: neap tides hardly rose
to springs at all. We had nothing to do, but plenty to
eat, for the river mouth at that time of year was full of
the finest sea-run whitefish. It was a good time for reading or lying on the deck in the September sun: well to
the north though we were, the wind for a few days was
changing that bleak country into a southland.

At last the gale blew itself out. We had now missed
springs and with each successive day, high water was
giving us less depth on the bar. If we did not wish to
wait for another ten days, which might mean northern
storms and even freeze-up, we had to get out.

The old *Emilia* was rigged with sails, one on her fore-
mast and another on her mizzen: she could not be called
schooner, ketch or anything in particular, she just had
sails. The skipper thought that the combined efforts of
steam and sail might get her over the bar. Her engines
were in her stern and as she was light, she was down by
the stern, which was the part of her that might strike.
To level her up, the skipper marshalled every one except
the operating hands on to the top of the high fo'c'stle. I

particularly remember Charlie, the Newfoundland
steward-cook, becoming valiant and lugging up with him
a spare anchor weighing a couple of hundred pounds.

The *Emilia* got her hook up, turned about and charg-
ed the bar. At the appropriate moment, the skipper gave
the word and up went the two big sails. She moved
majestically onward, doing her proud ten knots. Suddenly there was a terrific bump, repeated several times. The
stern came up and up, but we continued to go forward.
Then, like an object falling off a shelf, the stern dropped.
We were over!

It was a few hours more than an overnight's run over
to Stratton Island. When I woke up and crawled out of
my coalhole, we were already taking on stores at the
company's warehouse.

"What time did we get in?" I asked Charlie.

"Oh, about five o'clock. Didn't you hear him whistle?"

"No."

"Neither did I. He didn't. Just crept up quiet, let
go his hook and went ashore. Wonder what he expected
to find going on there."

The "chief" had joined us. "Can't trust these here
breed women, I guess."

So that was that.

"He" could not have found anything that wounded
his honour going on, as no ructions followed. The "breed
woman" turned out to be a buxom, hearty wench, with
several tow-headed children about her. She was the
daughter of an old Scot, who had come out in his youth,
had never after been off the Bay, and had married "country style." This old man, who had spent his life as a company servant in humble capacities, gave me my first
glimpse of what European feudalism could be: his complete readiness to take orders, whatever the tone they
were given in, his subservience, his subjection to the will
of others, constituted a new human phenomenon for me,

product of our equalitarian North American way of life but I have often seen the same type of deportment since, across the ocean, sometimes on the continent, more frequently in England.

We lay over at Stratton for two or three days, and there we added to our company, the district manager for Revillon Frères, one whom I shall call M. Desroseaux. He was a character. He had been brought up in Paris, son, I judged, of quite wealthy parents, and was the first specimen of the Parisian man-about-town whom I had encountered. What brought him out to the bush, I did not find out: it may have been to learn the fur business "from the ground up," it may have been that his family wanted to get rid of him: I recall that he had a great deal to say of the good days when he had had a leading Paris actress as his mistress, and of how he used to write her songs for her. That may not have been mere idle boasting: he was an amusing and a versatile chap, and I hope he came through the next four years' unpleasantness with a whole skin though I have never seen or heard of him since. From him I learned the virtues of Gruyère cheese (of which he had a whole year's supply in hand) and red wine. He and his French mates round the Bay carried their good food and their good manners into the farthest wilderness with them.

At Stratton there is superlative trout fishing in the small lakes that cover the island. However, I was anxious to try a dip of the nets in the strait there, as Stratton is over on the east side of the Bay, where conditions are entirely different from the west coast. It is just on the edge of the Canadian Shield: consequently the country is hilly and the water may be deep. The Newfoundlanders were only too anxious to help me handle the nets: that made them feel at home. The amateur help I had had all summer had usually got the nets into hopeless snarls: these Newfoundlanders handled them, floats, sinkers and all, as easily as a young woman measuring off cloth at a dry-goods counter. We did not find many fish out there: the estuaries, were better for that. Anyway, the Newfoundlanders soon lost interest. The big ship had been in from St. John's and had left boxes of dried herring. My Newfoundland friends at once abandoned our delicious fresh trout and went about munching dried herring: that was real fish!

We left Stratton, everything closed up for the winter, and arrived at Moose without event. It was now the beginning of October, and though I knew now I would never be taking up my appointment in Hamburg, I still had two hundred miles of hard travel ahead of me, up the Moose River to the line. Even though my route did lie south, that would make it late enough. If I had been content to take the shore-route by canoe, with its orthodox mudsitting technique, I could have done the trip in four or five days. As it was, I had taken twelve. But I had blundered into a new world, with new personalities, new ranges of experience, so I think maybe it was worth it.

IX

The Sea of the North:
The Return from the Northern Sea

NOWADAYS, one may take a train from Toronto and in a little over a day be in Moosonee, the terminus on James Bay; or he could get there in three or four hours by flying: the distance is only seven hundred miles. In the old days, it was not so simple as that. After the Canadian National was built, going down to the Bay was not a great feat, but coming up was quite a different matter. If one chose the Albany route back, he had no portages to speak of, but he did have several hundred miles of swift current, which made hard paddling and drastically reduced the daily mileage. If he went by the Moose and its tributaries, he had two hundred miles of some pretty tough going. My intentions when I left having been to make the round trip, down by the Albany and back by the Moose, I was prepared to take what came, though not for quite as hard a trip as it turned out to be.

Arriving at Moose Factory was like entering the port of New York: you were aware that you were coming to a metropolitan centre. Moose Factory was the headquarters of the Bay. There the two fur-trade companies had some senior officials, and both Anglicans and Catholics had establishments. At one time, the Anglican bishop of Moosonee used to keep his residence at Moose Factory.

One of the occupants of this see, Bishop Horder was an outstanding man, and a scholar. When I was up on the Bay, although he had been dead fifty years, his memory was still green, and many stories continued to be told of him. I am happy to possess a copy of his *Cree Grammar,* given me by one of my missionary friends.

Around the Hudson's Bay establishment, Moose Factory proper, which lies on an island in the river mouth, the generations had gathered the little tributary life of the neighbourhood. It is strange how on this wilderness outpost, as at Albany, one at once felt the sense of historical continuity given by an existence already longer than that of any settlement in English Canada. There was a certain amount of cultivation about the post, and quite a few good gardens. I even saw a horse. The Revillon post was some distance away, on the left (or west) bank of the river, where the T. and N.O. Railway now terminates, at Moosonee. Here I joined forces with the party corresponding to my own, which had been looking into the fisheries of the east coast. We decided to attack the river in the one canoe. I had sold mine to the Revillon post manager at Albany, who had brought in an outboard engine for it, the very first gas engine on the Bay. I was consequently an extra hand in the other canoe. That made six in the party but the big canoe held us all and our load easily.

The leader of the east coast party was C. D. Melville, a wandering Englishman. He had two canoemen, a backcountry farmer-lumberjack-guide named MacNabb from near Pembroke, Ontario, and a French Indian half-breed, Angus Chevrier. We were taking two passengers, a Major Southey, who had been working for the Hudson's Bay, and another Englishman named Wilson. The sixth member was myself.

Melville was an intelligent, sensitive person. He had poked round the west and north for most of his life, but why, I did not discover. He had, for example, once spent three years alone on Great Bear Lake, and as far as I could gather, for no reason in particular. How he survived I cannot understand for as a woodsman he was helpless. We became great friends, were in the same service during the war, and it was a matter of regret to me to learn that in the great 'flu epidemic of 1918, he had been one of the victims.

Southey was of the family of Robert Southey, the 19th century poet. He had been in the Boer war and was now going out to rejoin the British army. On the Bay he had not measured up, I understood, and was a discard. He was of the officer and gentleman type for which, I am afraid, I have little admiration. Such men without having more than average intelligence and with educations of doubtful validity, nevertheless do have good manners and an indefinable air of status about them. Englishmen of the type have often found it easy to float through Canadian life: they cash in on snobbery. The other passenger, Wilson, was also a discard: he, however, was lower middle class, which made him another kind of discard. The main thing I remember about him was that he had to start the day with a shave, no matter how difficult the circumstances.

Melville used to compare Angus Chevrier to J. M. Barrie's Admirable Crichton, the butler who took charge and pulled the party through when it got shipwrecked, but who immediately fell back into his subordinate place on its rescue. I think that was going rather far, for, if I may say so, while the three Englishmen probably would have come to grief if left to themselves, the other three members of the party would have got through handily enough. Wilson, for example, discovered after we left the post that his grub had not been put in: this put us all on short rations for the trip. Melville could not carry a pack, or, perhaps, as leader did not think it the thing to do so. Southey's military training had not included the art of finding his way about and there was always the danger of his getting lost in the bush. This is not to detract from the reputation of Angus Chevrier: an illiterate backwoods breed, Angus, in his own environment, was a man of cheerful common sense, good judgment, courage, resource.

Throughout the lower reaches of its course, the Moose River runs in a valley of a mile or two in width. The country consists in clay lying on flat limestone. The river has scraped all the clay off the limestone and every year widens out its valley by gouging out the clay banks. As soon as the spring floods are over, the river, spread out over these immense limestone flats, virtually disappears, leaving only thin threads of water here and there: these often spread out into not much more than a smear. It was not a matter of paddling up this "river," but of walking up it, and carrying our immense canoe into the bargain. Our method was to search for the most promising lead, follow this up until it became too shallow to float the canoe and then carry to the next lead we could find. It was always difficult to decide whether to try merely easing the canoe forward over the rock or to unload and make a formal portage. Usually whichever choice we made turned out to have been the wrong one. It was hard work and we could only make a little over five miles a day.

The paradox about the Moose was that the farther upstream we got, the more water we found. The reason was plain: the banks were formed of more resistant material and the valley therefore narrower. This meant more paddling, less carrying.

Perhaps the most fatiguing bit of the journey was getting over the four-mile portage: a portage of that length is never a joke, especially if hilly, as this one was. And in addition it had not been used for a long time, so that it was full of windfalls: we cut out some of these, but to clear it would have taken too long, so we simply climbed over them as best we could: climbing over a windfall with a pack on your back, or, more awkward still, the canoe, was not fun. Yet it was proving practicable to carry the canoe with two men, though she was pretty heavy and her width made her unwieldy. But instead of having three shifts we had only two, for Melville just did not volunteer and Wilson soon gave out: this left the two men, Major Southey and myself. Southey and I carried together: he was beginning to get broken to this hard work by the end of the trip.

It was on the four-mile portage that the Major (or as MacNabb referred to him, "Major," as if he were a dog) displayed his unerring woodcraft. He had taken a load over while supper was cooking, and coming back, the dark fell. Then the moon rose full at our backs. We came into a little clearing, or burn, and going across it, could not at once find where the trail left it. We looked about for a minute, and then "Major" shouted triumphantly, "I have it!" and started off down the trail in the direction from which we had just come, with the moon full in his face.

By this time, food was beginning to get short. We set a little net overnight and got some fish, among others, a small sturgeon. It made excellent eating but unfortunately we were out of salt, and that took the fun out of it. A day or two later, when we were down pretty well to a diet of fish without salt and little else, a moose was spotted on the bank, half a mile away. He had two cows with him. Angus began to call him. He put his cows into the bush and then came forth to do battle. He spotted the strange object in the water, and appeared quite ready to take it on, but Angus did not think it safe to take a chance on his going away by approaching closer, so the rifles were produced. Melville had a Ross sporting rifle,

I had a Winchester. Angus fired the Ross, with which he had fallen in love (Melville gave it to him at the end of the trip—an example of that feudal paternalism by which his class has so often attached its dependents). We both shot at him and one of us hit him, possibly both. At any rate, he solved our food problem, and his horns later adorned the entrance to my summer cottage. I must admit that "frying the luscious steaks over the fire" as they used to do in the boy's adventure books, was not quite all it might have been, for the meat, being so fresh, was tough as old boots.

Before leaving Moose Factory, I had become the proud possessor of a pair of high moose-skin boots. They came nearly up to my knees but the difficulty was that we were in and out of the water so much—more often than not over the waist rather than merely over the boot tops—that they were chronically full. Trying to dry them out one night, I scorched them. In two days the rocks had begun to disintegrate them and I looked forward to finishing our voyage barefoot, with bleeding feet. But on the next portage—and remember, the route bore no evidence of having been used in months—I found of all things . . . a pair of discarded boots! They were rather stylish for the bush, but they fitted me perfectly!

The hardest phase of our journey, by long odds, was the passage of the Victoria rapids. These are reckoned only as swift water, and thus not supposed to require a portage, but although they are several miles in length, it would probably have been better to force our way along the bank, or even to cut a trail. The rapids are made by the constricted river forcing itself over a smooth limestone bed, which is full of holes and ledges. We would pole our big canoe up the side eddies, then cautiously edge out round a point into the current, and paddle for all we were worth to get to the next eddy. Where the water ripped down past the points too quick for paddling, we had to

wade her up. The bowsman would get out, lower himself cautiously over the side until he got his feet on the
bottom and hold her, while the others cautiously edged
her forward. The trick was to feel with your feet and
find one of the potholes worn in the limestone by wandering granite boulders: this gave a foothold. She was edged
forward as far as safe, the bowsman would wade up to
the bow again and hold. The others would pile in and
grab paddles and poles. Often as the canoe would swing
as one was hanging on to her, his feet would go down
into deep water and if he had lost his hold of the canoe,
he would have had to swim the rapids, boots and all.
But you just hung on at such times until the forward men
had got her ahead a bit, when you usually were able to
get your feet down to the bottom again.

We were wet from head to foot whole October days,
and October is a bit late in the year to be wet all day.
I did not find that going to sleep more or less wet, which
I invariably did, worked me any harm: I had plenty of
blankets and the warmth of my body soon dried me out.
It is, in fact, with some hestitation that I set down such
experiences as these, lest they be taken as "hardships:"
they cannot be considered such, in view of the infinite
burden of suffering that mankind has borne since those
days.

At the end of the second week, we reckoned we must
be close to "the line." A little later, rounding a bend, we
saw a log shack standing in a little clearing with cows in
it. The shack was symbolical, for behind it were ranged,
not Indian trappers but all the farmlands of North
America, with cities, schools, churches; all the apparatus
of our society marched in the rear of that shack. "And
if he gets the little woman in there, they'll be happy as
larks," sang out MacNabb, the only man among us who
was himself a member of the order of farmer-frontiers-
men.

The clearing, of course, settled the matter: we were close to "the steel." A few miles more and we reached it, coming in at Fauquier, on the Groundhog river, a branch of the Metagami. Few people who have never been out of country served by the railway can conjure up what it means to come upon it again out of the bush. The bush is like the sea and coming to the railway is like making a landfall.

The manager of the experimental farm at Fauquier showed us the prize potatoes he had grown: we were indeed out of the woods. A whistle was heard, wheels ground to a stop, we piled aboard. My summer's Odyssey was over.

X

How the News Was Heard:
Two Wars and a Peace

IT WAS the early autumn of 1914. For several months I had been far away in the north, quite out of touch with "civilization," to report on the possibilities of commercial fishing in James Bay. By midsummer, I had worked up to the north tip of the west coast. From that point I had begun my return, and about the middle of September had reached the Albany river, which had been my point of departure for the north, and from which my journey back to southern Canada would begin.

Since there was no radio in those days, anyone going into the bush anywhere was cut off from the outside world as soon as he left "the steel." During the season of open water, a post like Albany, at the mouth of the river, would get news whenever any party of Indians or of officials came down the river from "the line." This might happen two or three times a season. In 1914, the only party to come down, in addition to my own, had left the line at the end of the first week in August.

The little settlement at Albany lay a few miles up the river, on the north shore. We paddled along under the bank until we came to the Hudson's Bay Company's landing. Grounding the canoe, I stepped out and began to walk up the bank. Mr. Gillies, the factor, came down to meet me.

"Well, you're back a little sooner than you thought."

"No, just about the time I calculated on. Don't you remember I told you when I left that I would have to be back in good time. I hope you have some news for me: I was expecting letters here which would help me decide when I should leave the Bay and strike for 'the line'."

"Oh, yes, of course, you were planning to go over to Germany this fall, weren't you." (I had accepted a post as lecturer in the Hamburg Colonial Institute.)

"Yes, to Hamburg. If I'm to get there on time, I'll have to be making tracks, won't I?"

"Yes, but you needn't be in any hurry."

"But surely I do need to be, to get out to 'the line' and across the ocean within two or three weeks."

"Well, you won't be going to Germany. Not just yet, anyway."

"Why not? How do you know?"

"Haven't you heard the news? I thought that's what brought you back."

"No, I've heard no news: how could I?"

"Well, you won't be going to Germany. Great things have happened since you left here."

"Oh, what kind of things?"

"We're at war with Germany."

Just like that! Out of a blue sky. Not the slightest preliminary. No bulletins, no special editions, no apprehensions, no crowds in the streets. Just "we're at war with Germany" six weeks after the event. For me that's the way the earthquake occurred. Just a single sentence, but one that broke the isolation of that northern world in which I was and of all other peaceful communities forever and forever.

"We're at war with Germany."

There were no details available. During the six weeks anything might have happened. The next leg of my journey took me over to Moose Factory. No further word there. My friend Desroseaux of Revillons, who was a French reservist and was going out as soon as he could in order to return to France, had armed himself with two big jack-knives from company stores. "They'll be fine for cutting up a bullock in the field," he explained.

From Moose I plunged into the bush again, on my way up the river to "the line," which I reached on October 14th. At Fauquier, the point at which I hit it, the postmaster, in the unconventional way of the north, obligingly handed out to me all the newspapers in his office, however addressed. I read them with avidity, and the whole vast surge of the thing spread out before me. War had always seemed to me something unreal, a matter of "unhappy far-off things." Now, in loudest of accents, it was upon us. Four months before I had left a peaceful world—at least my corner of it had been peaceful. I had not even heard of the events at Sarajevo (June 28th). And now this, the world aflame. It was the biggest job in mental adjustment that I have ever had to face.

.   .   .   .   .

For me, the war's end was scarcely less personal. I had been home on leave and was on my way back across the Atlantic to join my ship, which I had left at Dover. I was crossing on what is known in the Service as an "indulgence passage" (by which you pay a stated daily rate), and was sailing by the Union Castle liner *Durham Castle*. We left Quebec at the beginning of November, as a member of a big convoy, with a cruiser escort. The enemy had begun to wobble and one sensed that the end was not too far off, but it will be recalled that in 1918 the collapse was more sudden than in 1945, so that there was no immediate suggestion that the fight was about over.

The word went round, however, that the *Durham Castle* had been sent to embark American troops and that their sailing had been cancelled. The ship was empty, anyway. That surely was a sign.

We were, of course, in touch by wireless, but for safety's sake, our ship did not use hers, messages being signalled from the cruiser. All the indulgence passengers (there were no others) being nobodies, they were not kept informed; what news they got drifted down from the bridge to that ship's gossip, the purser, and thence outward from him.

On November 9th, 1918, when half-way across, the purser passed on a message, "straight from the cruiser's bridge," so to speak. It certainly was an exciting message. The war had ended. Fritz had crumpled up. An English major aboard, who had fought the war on the flying fields of Canada, expanded and ordered champagne all round. There being only nine of us in the enormous dining-saloon, we could not work up a very riotous celebration. Moreover, we had just disposed of the major's champagne when the purser reported that he had been in error: the war had not ended. Fritz had not crumpled up. We all then went quietly about our business, and the ship's deadlights were duly put in place that night, as before. Lookouts still strained through the darkness for submarines.

Two days later, the purser had more news. It was November 11th, the day of the armistice. This time, however, we were inclined to take the purser's news with a grain of salt: the major did not order champagne. We decided to wait and see. As the day wore on, it became more and more apparent that there must have been something in the purser's report. Little relaxation began to appear, further crumbs of news to trickle through from the bridge. By nightfall we were beginning to believe

that the war was about over. The cruiser's masthead
morse-signal light flashed just close enough to dusk to
make us fancy that she was not worrying too much.

The next day, the purser came up with the rumour
that we had spoken with a couple of German submarines:
they had heard, too, and were heading back to their base.
Whatever the relations between us and them, if we really
had intercepted some message from them, it didn't look
as if we were enemies in the old mortal sense. By nightfall,
more word had come, rumours proved correct and, though
war-time regulations were still maintained, the tension
had eased. Yet it was difficult to realize that that night
men would no longer be killing one another.

As the war began for me, so it had ended. I missed
all the shouting, all the delirium of the armistice, all the
public celebrations. My war was a personal war, begun
and ended in relative loneliness.

·   ·   ·   ·   ·

Twenty-five years after that first fatal interruption to
the world's peace, I was again on salt water, this time
in a little thirty-footer on the coast of Nova Scotia, for
what I call my own pleasure. I had with me a young man
from Halifax, who, besides being a good sailor and a good
companion, was a mechanical wizard. There was an old
car radio aboard, run off the battery of the auxiliary
engine. I had long since given it up as hopeless, but he
sat down and fiddled with it for a few hours, turned the
knobs, and there was music!

The other member of my crew was a young fellow
from Lunenburg. He was a good lad and had taken
wireless courses, but had been unable to find a job afloat,
and was putting in time as a paid hand (very badly paid)
on my little sloop. His father was captain of a "banker"
and had always discouraged him from learning to sail:
that was a curse which lay heavy enough on the family

already, he seemed to think. So the boy was sent on to school, and though familiar with the water, as every mother's son in Lunenburg is, he was no sailor.

We were running down the coast to Mahone Bay and had got in behind the Sambro Ledges, creeping slowly through the fog. We lay up for the night behind Little Sambro Island. While the boys rowed off to Sambro village for some supplies, I walked about the island. On the outer side, a dozen feet above high water, lay rows of great boulders, some of them a foot in diameter, yet worn to smooth balls and tossed to this enormous height by the fury of the winter storms. The other side of the island, open to the long Atlantic swell, was no place for a small boat to lie at anchor. That was evident.

I went back on board, and, as I waited for the young men, turned on the mended radio. Voices poured out, excited voices, angry voices, frightened voices. For it was the first week of September in that year of fate, 1939. Here was our little vessel lying safe under Sambro Island, with the long sweep of the Atlantic barred out by the island's bulk. But the ship of the world was out in the storms, with no captain on the bridge: rather, it seemed, madmen, or well-intentioned weaklings. Poor ship, it was labouring now, and the waves were hissing white as they came aboard. What the end of it would be who could tell?

So there I was, alone in the cabin of a little yacht, solitary in the Atlantic, just as before I had been solitary, or almost solitary, in the north at the first storm's opening and in mid-ocean for its end. As I listened, with the full meaning of the horror coming in on me, the young men came back. We had all been expecting the blow to fall, of course, and now they, along with me, were hearing it descend. There was no thought on their part that Canada would be out of it. In their minds both were already in it. They had no reflections to make and no political interests: excitement buoyed them up and they looked forward to adventure. The young Lunenburger would be away in a matter of days to find a ship and operate a key. The young fellow from Halifax was determined to get into the air force.

The next day we finished our voyage, and parted. I have never heard a word from either of them since. Good airman and good wireless operator, I am sure they made. Where are they now, I wonder.

XI

From Boston to Bremen on the Good Ship "Jeannette Skinner"

THERE surely can be few more boring experiences than crossing the ocean on a liner. On a liner you are as far removed from sea as is a lady's hat from utility. No doubt the hat has some sort of relationship to clothing and the passenger on a liner to the sea, but the connection in both cases is tenuous. The sea, it might be said, is barely visible from the decks of a liner—which are always crowded with silly people who don't know one end of a ship from the other and regard an ocean passage as nothing but shuffleboard, or worse, bridge and booze. Anyone who loves the sea will hate the liner.

In the palmy days when everyone, speaking figuratively, was crossing the ocean, myself included, I found out that I could get across on a freighter. By going in her, my passage would cost me little more than my board and I would avoid the liner's passengers. It is true that I would have to go to Germany, whereas my destination was England, but she would get me across, I would have twelve days at sea, with the run of the ship open to me and the feel of her under me. On liners, the ship's company scuttle away like frightened rabbits from all passengers except pretty ladies, and well they may, but aboard the freighter I would be a member of the ship's company.

71

The *Jeannette Skinner* was lying at one of the wharves in East Boston. I put my baggage aboard and sought out the captain. "You'll have to sign on," he said, "we aren't licensed to carry passengers."

"All right," I replied, "in what capacity?"

"Oh, we'll put you down as a deckhand and your wages will be one cent a month."

"You can't expect much work for that."

"I don't."

A major problem arose at once. Where was I to sleep? "There aren't any extra cabins on her," said the captain. "I guess we'll have to put you in the slop-chest."

That sounded ominous. But the "slop-chest" turned out to be just an extra cabin after all. They took out the "slops," which are oil-skins, sea-boats and other such gear, kept for issue *en route,* and I was comfortable enough. There was no bath on board, so I used a hose on deck. The dining-saloon was just beside my door: the food was not for pernickety men, but it was good enough, and plentiful.

The *Jeannette Skinner* was chartered by the American government to a private operating company. Like most other American ships in those days, few of which could accomplish the feat of carrying a cargo over the American tariff wall, she never paid even her operating costs: the department of government concerned probably welcomed my widow's mite. One of the ship's officers told me that on one trip they had had prospects of a full cargo of Belgian glass but before they could load, a presidential order appeared, and up went the tariff: the cargo of glass was not shipped. He thought some American glass firm had got wind of the pending import. The arrangement which kept the ship steaming backward and forward across the ocean in dignified emptiness was simple, and unique: the government paid the operating company the balance between earnings and costs, plus a percentage on the difference. That particular trip must have cost it even more than usual. "The company make their money on their losses" was the way the officer put it.

Two days out from Boston brought us into warmer weather and the easterly traffic lane. By that time I was well acquainted with all the mess, the captain, three mates, three engineers and the wireless operator. They were a rich and rare company. The second engineer was from Lowell, Mass. His people, he said, had come from England when Lowell was growing up into a textile town, a century and a quarter before. Between him and the old stock Yankees, it seemed a big gulf still stretched. The first engineer was an Englishman of Dutch extraction, and the "chief", a Norwegian: no blue-eyed Viking giant, but one of the little dark "sawed offs" from the coastal rim. The second and third mates, like the skipper, were from Maine. The second mate was slight and balding, and, contrary to the run of men at sea, puritanical. He was constantly deploring the behaviour of his mates ashore. This he might have carried off, had he been a man of some weight, which he was not. I must say, however, that his exhortations against wine and women were taken good-humouredly enough and earned him nothing worse than occasional practical jokes.

The wireless operator, or "Sparks," as these gentlemen are universally called at sea, was "Boston Irish:" a good sort, but rather "mouthy." He was the first man I ever encountered who referred to the English as "limies": I had not known before that it was a general American sea term.

The real gem was the first mate, Chief Officer Macshane, a Nova Scotian of French Canadian and Irish parentage. He had a hand as big as both of mine, a frank, slow manner, complete self-assurance joined with simplicity, and a fund of good stories. He handled men sailing-ship fashion. "See that fellow down there, a-sweepin'," he would say to me: "Sea-lawyer. Come and argued with me, he did. Brought another along of him. I laid him out." He meant it. "Laying men out" had been routine for mates in the old days of sail, those days when men were yoked to the cruellest of callings for six months at a time and only iron discipline would bring them through privation and tempest.

The first engineer was the ship's intellectual: he read. And he had a thin atmosphere of sophistication about him. "Well," he had remarked, looking at me as if I were some strange new kind of beast, "You're a professor: I've often wondered what a professor would look like." He indicated that he was intrigued at the new experience, and somewhat flattered, which surely was an unusual note. Poor fellow, no one took him very seriously, and to his own misfortune, he was always falling foul of the first mate.

One morning we were at breakfast. Macshane, as was his duty, had "the hands" employed about the deck. The landsman may not think there is much to do aboard ship at sea, but on that voyage, the *Jeannette Skinner* was "chipped down" from stem to stern (which means that with chisel and hammer, the crew chipped all the old paint and rust off her decks) and repainted. On the morning in question, "chipping-down" was going on lustily just outside the saloon. There was a noise like a boiler factory. Conversation was impossible.

"Confound the row," said the first engineer, who liked to talk. He glanced significantly in the direction of the mate, got up and slammed the door.

"You t'ink mebbe work shouldn't be done, eh?" said Chief Officer Macshane.

"I think nothing of the sort. I merely closed the door," replied the engineer. He was not one of those who are "ware of entrance to a quarrel."

"You close the door, eh?"

"Sure, I closed the door."

The mate smoldered. At last he burst out:

"You start chippin' in the engine-room at four o'clock and the t'ird mate, he couldn't sleep. The Captain have to come and tell you to stop." (At four, the third mate would have just come off watch).

This was argument, not exactly battle, so the first engineer, summoning his wits, replied, though rather weakly, that that was the business of "the chief," his boss.

"Yes, but you start it and you have to stop it, and now you make row because my men chip at breakfast time. Huh!" The "huh" efficiently expressed sarcasm and contempt.

"I made no row, I simply closed the door:" the engineer was standing on his dignity, a precarious position for the likes of him.

"The work's gotta be done. Can't do work like that wit'out a noise." Here the mate addressed the ceiling: "Makin' a row because work's goin' on!"

The exchange of salvos ended, the engineer subdued by the ominous glower from the direction of the mate. A strained silence set in, third parties present looking at their plates and saying nothing. The mate, having finished his breakfast, sat there glaring at the engineer's plate. The mess boy came in, pushing the door open again. This time the engineer did not close it. The noise outside was as loud as ever.

The engineer, having swallowed the rest of his breakfast, got up and left.

"Huh!" said the mate, and left too.

Macshane and I became great friends, and he promised to show me the sights when we got to Bremen. I accepted the invitation with some mental reservations. As for the rest, four days out they had quit talking in homesick fashion of Boston and all the beer they had drunk there, and were beginning to talk of how bored

they were with the trip and of all the beer they were
going to drink in Bremen. And for sailors this is mainly
what the sea represents: long periods of ennui, cooped up
with accidental companions, away from home and family,
periods of ennui broken at intervals by sad gaiety in their
ports of call.

In due course we made our landfall off Cornwall, and
went on up the English Channel. It was in June, the air
was warm, the coast of England clear as a bell. One
could see woods, churches, houses, for we were only three
or four miles off the headlands. How small the experience
made the island seem! From the Atlantic, we had, as
sailors say, "brought up" the land at daylight and by
dark of that long evening, we were nosing out into the
North Sea. I remember with especial clarity, Folkestone
(which was really where I was supposed to be going),
Dover, Deal and the Goodwins, for in those waters, I had
passed night after dark night during the winters of the
first World War.

The North Sea was as quiet as a millpond. We coasted
the flat shores of Holland and the Frisian Islands, ticking
off the lightships one by one. They might have been a
hundred miles at sea for any land there was in sight. And
yet it was there, just a few miles off to starboard.

At one lightship we turned in a right angle, eight
points to starboard: this was the entrance to the River
Weser and the great port of Bremen. The lightship faded
from our sight before land began to show up, and then
there was nothing but sand and mud banks. We spoke
a pilot cutter. The pilots were the first Germans in
nautical uniform I had seen since we took the surrender
of their submarines at the close of the war. It gave me a
queer feeling to behold the ex-enemy whom I had never
seen while fighting with him, something like having a live
knight step out of a suit of armour.

It took an interminable time to crawl in out of the North Sea up the Weser, past endless dockyards, past Bremerhafen, to Bremen itself. At one point in the river, the great German liner *Europa* was lying, in a slip scarcely longer than herself, and into that little space she had been launched. How had they stopped her, after she rushed down the ways?

Arrived and docked, I thought I would catch the evening train for Berlin. "Oh, no," said the captain, "you are a member of the crew; you must be properly discharged, otherwise you will be a deserter." So I had to wait until morning and go with him to the consul's office, where I ceremoniously received my discharge and gave a receipt for my wages, my precious one cent.

Then I could go back and take my leave of my friends. "I've often thought I'd like to go to Berlin," said the second engineer. "Why don't you?" I asked, well knowing that no sailor ever leaves a port: he knows no more of the countries he visits than the little bridgehead round the docks that he builds out from his ship.

"Drink a 'kleine' for me in Berlin," called the first engineer, showing off to the last. I suppose he really meant a "grosse" a big one, not "a small one."

And so I left them. Shipmates of mine, they had been. And good shipmates, too.

XII

Across the Atlantic on 15,000 Tons of High Explosive

THE dock warehouse at Montreal teemed with activity. Countless men with electric trucks and hand-trucks wheeled innumerable bags and packages out to the docksides, whence they were swung to the decks of the steamer alongside, there to disappear through those yawning holes, her hatches. Trucks, winches, winchcables and men combined to produce a high, regular note, as constant as the orderly confusion of the scene.

It was a spring night in one of the early years of the First World War. On the ship's great bows stood out the letters R U S S I A N. This was her name, not her nationality. She was, in fact a British passenger freighter of the old Leyland Line, loading explosive from Canadian mills for Allied guns.

I went aboard her. I had a right to do so, for I was being given a passage in her. I was in civilian clothes but not for much longer. I was on my way across the ocean to join what every Canadian referred to simply as "The Navy," meaning the British Navy (in those days the Canadian Navy hardly existed). The opportunity had come to a number of young Canadians to serve with the British. I was one of them. I regarded myself as lucky. Like so many other young fellows whose "teens" had coincided with the early century, I had been brought up in the faith, the proud naval faith that radiated out from Great Britain to her colonies. The first book I can remember reading was G. A. Henty's *Under Drake's Flag:* I can still close my eyes and see those convoys of Spanish galleons, those daring boarding parties, cutlasses in teeth, swarming from Drake's ships over their sides. Drake, Nelson and the rest were in those days our living Canadian tradition.

Tradition had been reinforced by environment. For a youngster a Canadian lake is no bad substitute for the sea. It is a good place to play at pirates and to learn to handle boats. I can remember crossing Kempenfelt Bay once in the old days in such a pirate ship, a "ship" which was, in fact, a leaky old row boat that we had to bail constantly and vigorously to keep afloat. Still earlier memories take me back to days when as a child I learned to row. Then there were the games when the skiff was a liner and myself and playmates her captain and crew, bringing her alongside her berth (a log on the beach) with what skill we could.

And now the hour was come to some of us, a few chosen spirits we considered ourselves, to enter the proud force which had helped supply whatever *esprit de corps* we as colonials could have. There have always been in Canada great numbers of young men who, either by their way of life as lumbermen, fishermen, bushmen and so on, or because of the summer water tradition which is so strong amongst us, have been competent in all the skills of the small craft, in canoes and rowboats, dinghies, sloops, tugs and launches. Those who have had opportunity to test their skill on the high seas, who have known a craft large enough to sleep upon, have been relatively few. I was now to join this familiar Canadian small craft skill to the real thing, the sea-going ship, the ship of war. It was a big moment, and there would have been little point in talking to me of the horrors of war.

I was given a cabin upon the upper deck, just above
the bridge. The ship sailed during the night and in the
morning I had a sight of the other men who were going
over for the same purpose as myself. I should explain
that the Canadians who were selected for the Royal Navy
were sent over in small drafts; reflecting the movements
of the selection officers about the country. On board the
Russian, there were only nine of us all told, two going
over to become engineers, the rest deck officers.

They were a mixed lot. Four of them were definitely
"class;" in fact, I discovered for the first time that there
were people in Canada who were well beyond the
ordinary reach and quite conscious of that fact. Three
of these four had been members of a well-known Canadian yacht club, the fourth was a member of a prominent
Conservative family. They were, in fact, all Conservatives
and Anglicans. For them, going to join the Royal Navy
was in a sense a social act, rather than something romantic
and historical as it was for me.

One of the others was an Englishman who had
originally gone overseas with the Canadian army and
then had been returned to Canada. He claimed to have
been invalided out, though it soon became fairly evident
that the demon rum had had something to do with whatever it was that had happened to him. He was a ne'er-
do-well and an egotist, the kind of egotist rarely produced
in this simple country. For those foolish enough to listen
to him, he had been everywhere and knew all the ropes.
He had seen all the horrors of war and all the more
dreadful occurrences which, in the First World War, used
to be rumoured as having actually taken place. For example, it was reported from time to time that a Canadian
soldier had been crucified by the Germans: this chap had
seen it done.

The drunken egotist soon ceased to count for much
among us and might be dismissed were it not for the

plight into which he later on got another of the group. This was a poor, sad fellow from Toronto, a man then middle-aged who in civil life had sold men's clothing in a Toronto department store. He used to emphasize to the rest of us what a privilege it was for humble people like ourselves to be taken into the British navy. His only claim to special qualification for a place in the navy had been a few vacations cruising Lake Ontario in small boats belonging to his friends. He was a decent sort of fellow, a natural gentleman, but with nothing more than the humblest of educations and, unfortunately, too large a thirst. When we had completed the trip and had all been housed at Greenwich Naval College, on the very first night there, this poor fellow did not turn up at the hour prescribed for cadets to be "aboard," ten o'clock. In fact he did not turn up at all, but about two o'clock in the morning, the august Admiral in command of the College was awakened by his telephone bell ringing and found that it was the London police on the other end of the line. They told him they had a man there, drunk and more or less disorderly, in civilian clothes, who claimed to be "a British naval officer" living in Greenwich Naval College. They were told rather tartly to keep him there and send him out the next morning. At that time there duly arrived our friend, a much sadder and wiser man. It seems that the ne'er-do-well Englishman had volunteered to show him the sights of London and then, after they had both had a good many too many, had become a bit noisy, had left him in the lurch and the police had taken him in. He fully expected to be dismissed the service on the spot, but the Admiral was understanding and let him off with a warning and some stoppage of leave. He and I became quite good friends later on: I remember how I used to slave of an evening, when we were studying navigation, trying to explain to him what an angle was.

There was another curious chap, also from Toronto, whose nautical experience had been confined, apparently, to taking what he always referred to as a "one and a half horse" from Toronto to Oakville and back. He, too, had had no formal education, but he was much more confident of himself than the clothing salesman, accustomed to knocking about outdoors and thus with a little more assurance than can be got from serving behind a counter. After we had all received our training, this man was dispatched to Portsmouth, to await posting to a ship. At Portsmouth, he was told that he would live in one of the "hulks" there used as barracks and in due course a boat was sent off from her to fetch him. In the navy an officer's taking over from its coxswain a boat sent ashore to embark him is an act of ceremony and ritual. The men sit with oars up-ended or "tossed," the officer steps in, places himself in the stern sheets and gives the necessary commands, which result in the oars being laid in the water and struck in unison. Our friend found the situation a bit novel, for at that period of his training he knew little of naval etiquette. Nothing happening, as he took his seat, the oars continuing to be held aloft, he blurted out, "What the — are you holding those things up there for: get them into the water and get out of here." Which the boat's crew proceeded to do. I wonder what the shade of Nelson whispered to them as they rowed past the *Victory*. Probably "I didn't have any colonial officers to deal with in my day."

The man I chummed up with came from Picton. I can see now why we became chums: we were both middle class. That also does not sound very Canadian, but the explanation will nevertheless hold for considerable areas in Canadian life. This chap had no airs, he had a fair education, plenty of intelligence and initiative: he was what people would call "a typical Canadian," with neither the sense of exclusiveness clothing the ex-members of the well-known yacht club, nor the brashness and vulgarity of our friend of the boat's crew incident. A third man of the type was going over to be an engineer: unfortunately that would only rate him a chief petty officer's status, so that while we were still all in civilian clothing, the almost insurmountable English barrier between officers and "lower deck" was beginning to go up.

The *Russian* took out the largest cargo at the deepest draft of any ship that up to that period had gone down the St. Lawrence. It was whispered about that at some points she hardly cleared the bottom of the channel by more than a few inches. And her cargo was almost exclusively—high explosive!

Fifteen thousand tons of T.N.T. with enough fulminate of mercury to detonate it as the foundation for one's bed was not exactly what the average man would have chosen, especially for a trip across the Atlantic and more especially still in war time, when a torpedo, or a shot, would have sent the whole business sky-high. However, it would have made a good, loud bang and would not have lasted long. I did not encounter anyone on board who lost any sleep about such possibilities.

We put into Sydney, Nova Scotia, for coal. Everybody went ashore and the two conspicuously thirsty members of the party, the pair referred to above, immediately sought a drink. Sydney was "dry" in those days, but someone employed the standard device for getting a drink in a dry town—they asked a policeman where to go. He obligingly told them.

The captain gave us the run of his ship, so that I was able to follow through the daily routine, from the morning "sight" for time, and hence for longitude, around through the noon "sight" for latitude and on to the afternoon "sight" for longitude again. Bells, watches, coxswains, tricks at the wheel, the niceties of rank, both on deck and in the dining saloon, all these, so far away from the experience of the Canadian inlander, began to take on familiarity and to be accepted as matters of course. As a result of our voyage some useful steps in our naval education had already been completed before we formally entered for naval training.

There were only two occasions during the voyage itself when I got any feeling—as apart from knowledge—that we were on the high seas in wartime and therefore always in a state of considerable danger. One was when "the Chief" (Chief Engineer) took us down below to show off his engines and, opening a little steel bulkhead door at the after end of his engine room, stepped through it, beckoned to a couple of us to follow him and then shut the door carefully behind us. We had been ushered into "the tunnel," the long shoulder-high, steel arch, shaped like an inverted "U," built over the shaft from where it leaves the engine room to the point at which it passes through the hull to receive the propellor. There we were, thirty feet down below the surface, with a fraction of an inch of steel plate between us and the cold, deep ocean, the noise of the propeller crashing in our ears as it shoved the whole vast ship along, the shaft spinning merrily around, with jets of water playing on its bearings and the whole brilliantly illuminated, a tight, closed little world of our own, which nevertheless would have spelled certain, and unfortunately, somewhat lingering death for us if an enemy torpedo had chanced to strike. That scene often recurred to me as I went through the war. As the tale of sinkings by submarine mounted and so many brave fellows died down underneath in their little steel compartments, that scene prodded my imagination with an additional touch of realism. It reinforced the little streak of claustrophobia which inheres in me, I suppose, a streak in my psychology that would have deterred me from submarine service, for example. There were never any terrors for me at sea as long as I stood up in the air, with the blue of sea and sky about me. Those two blues seem for me to make things completely as they should be, the safest of heavens above and the most natural of floors beneath, the sea floor, more natural and more solid. if it could be, than that of earth itself. But to be caught far down below, surrounded by steel barriers of the race's own making, miserably suffocated or drowned by inches, as some of the men I knew were when their submarines failed to rise again, that, somehow, for me seems to carry horror beyond the endurable.

The second occasion was on the surface: it was therefore merely exciting. Two days off Ireland a trail of smoke appeared on the eastern horizon. It approached. As it changed into a ship, its silhouette revealed a fighter. The captain seemed anxious. As we watched, another trail appeared and another fighter materialized. A signal was made, the captain's anxiety relaxed. Two British destroyers to convoy us in. "Before we got his signal," said the captain, "I thought he might have been a raider: he didn't hit us quite on the nail, you know." The thought had not occurred to the irresponsibles who were his passengers: we had just watched ships approaching.

The day was clear and blue, the wind strong from the southwest, the sea long and steady and high. The destroyers, as they pranced about us, sometimes were almost hidden by the crests of intervening waves. At other times, as they turned, they seemed almost like flies crawling up a wall. They assumed every position except riding with their smoke stacks immersed. We, on the good old *Russian*, with our fifteen thousand tons of T.N.T., were safe and steady. "They'll get their soup spilled for them today," said the captain, jerking his thumb in the direction of one of them, as she did a nose dive down a wave.

Destroyers are most uncomfortable craft. They are light. They shiver in any wind. And they are fast: they charge at, over and through the waves. They move in every direction at once. Most men get used to them in time but the occasional individual has a curse upon him and can never accommodate his stomach to the motion. This has no bearing on his capacity as a seaman. A destroyer captain I once knew told me that at that time he had been twenty-seven years at sea and seldom was able to sit through an entire meal below. This situation comes as close to abstract hell as can well be found on earth.

Even so, no comparison can properly be made between the lot of the sailor in war time and that of the soldier, especially the P.B.I. At sea, nine days out of ten, you are comfortable and well fed, even if tired and on occasion wet. Bursts of action are few and far between. When they come they may mean total loss such as is seldom experienced on land; in both wars the naval ratio of "killed in action" was relatively high, even as compared with the army's. Of course "killed in action" more often than not means "drowned in action." Be that as it may, as a brother officer of mine once put it to a Frenchman in trying to explain the difference in his lot as a sailor and his former sad estate when in the army: "J'ai mon lit" —"I have my bed." Those words in war mean a tremendous lot. No sailor, or ex-sailor, would ever claim that his lot compared in suffering with that of the infantryman, immersed for days, may be, as many of ours were in both wars, in slush and mud and blood.

Taking sights, scribbling down figures, doing sums and coming up with the words "that's where we are," making at the same time a little cross on the chart, all seem the height of mystery to the landsman. Such things —the short term for them is navigation—are not really as mysterious as they seem, especially as much of the navigator's work has been done for him years before in the astronomical observatories and their attendant offices. After all, it is not the sailor who finds out exactly where the planet Venus is going to be in the heavens, ten years from tonight at seven minutes past eleven. Nor was it simple sailors who made that instrument of precision, the sextant, nor even those ingenious practical devices, the parallel rulers and the dividers. The making of charts is itself an exact science, with several centuries of history behind it. The practical sailor profits, like every other practical man, from the accumulated technique of civilization.

When, one day, I saw the Third Officer doing his little sums, consulting his Nautical Almanac in the process, I asked him "What would you do if you lost your books?" He answered simply, "I'd borrow someone else's." "But supposing there were no books available." "Then we'd be beat," he said. There is no known method, so far as I know, of working out astronomical tables in your head. I suppose a seafarer of long experience, by taking a good look at the sun, can tell how many degrees it is above the horizon at noon, and therefore make a shrewd guess at the latitude, but even such a man is helpless on longitude, unless he is carrying Greenwich Mean Time around with him, which means a chronometer, or at the very least a good watch. Of course, no good sailor is entirely dependent on the last word in technical sophistication. After all Columbus got across the ocean with compass alone, plus a crude affair for taking the sun's level known as "the sticks," and farther back than that, the Norsemen got to America without even a compass. But a modern big ship—especially one loaded with high explosive—is a different proposition from a Viking long boat and has to be navigated with mathematical precision. After all, thanks to the men on shore, all the ship's officer has to know is the four simple rules of arithmetic and how to take figures out of a table. In the Navy, officers who are going to make a career of it get a very thorough mathematical grounding and know what the figures represent which they take out of tables, and how they got there, but not in the merchant service: everything there goes by rule, and goes very well, too.

Eventually we sighted our first light, the Tusket, off the southern coast of Ireland. Next day we brought up, as sailors say, the Scilly Islands (not in the way one might think he was doing when seasick), Land's End and in the afternoon, the famous Eddystone off Plymouth. At Plymouth we put in, making our way up the crowded harbour to the naval base of Devonport, where we docked. As we came alongside, we could see a warship in a dry dock at a distance, her upper works all battered. It was the famous *Barham*, here to lick her wounds after Jutland. The *Barham* was to serve many a year after that, remaining in service during much of the second war, eventually to blow up, in the Mediterranean, with loss of nearly all hands.

As I glanced through the port in my cabin, just before taking out my bag, a stream of water came in: it was nothing serious, merely the signal that we had arrived and that you could now be as casual as you liked: after all, even if it did drench bunk and blankets, "they" would fix it up. Going out on the deck, I saw a hatch cover off and two or three dockyard workers standing casually about. Eventually they got out a sack of some sort, hoisting it toward shore. As it hovered over the space between ship and quay, the sling holding it gave way and the bag fell down on the edge of the quay, breaking open. I don't know what was in it, some yellowish stuff, it may have been T.N.T. It didn't go off and the workers did not seem to make anything of the occurrence. I thought of the ordered, high pressure loading we had left behind us with the warehouse sheds at Montreal: at the dockyard workers' rate of going, the old *Russian* would be there for many a day.

We parted from her, taking our first step on English soil. As potential sailors were in duty bound to do, we set course at once for Drake's Plymouth Hoe.

Eventually they must have got the *Russian* unloaded for she was reported torpedoed.

Captain Dickinson and comrades, are you sleeping down below?

XIII

The Germans Raid the Straits

I AM of course, an outdated old back-number. My war was the First Great War—concluded in 1918, long before most of the present generation was born. Since then there has been another Great War and also a Small War. The Second Great War is already ancient history to the children of those who fought in it, while even the early veterans of the Small War are beginning to get the odd grey hair. So I am as remote as a veteran of Waterloo. That at least lends a kind of timelessness to me.

At any rate, may I inform you who are still living that in my war, I had various exciting passages and that we probably handled whatever situations we had to handle just as capably and as energetically as you are likely to do today. My own share was small but respectable: I helped man a small auxiliary patrol craft, operating mostly out of the ports of Dover, England, and Dunkerque, France. This auxiliary patrol ship was known technically as a "Motor Launch." But she was a rather overgrown launch, eighty feet by twelve, forty tons, six foot draft, twenty knots speed at her best, carrying three pounder "pop-gun," machine guns, depth charges—and a fuel supply of 2,000 gallons of gasoline. There was hardly an inch of her eighty feet, from stem to stern, which would not have become a blazing furnace if it had been properly and neatly hit! Strange to say, although these little ships were numerous, this never happened: for one thing, they were low in the water; poor marks, especially in a seaway.

Our complement was twelve men, two officers, two engineers, petty officer coxswain, seven seamen. We were all amateurs together, except a few of the coxswains, who had been fishermen—but not trained naval hands. As amateurs, we had to navigate, manage the ship in dirty weather, do mine-sweeping, run the engines, fire the gun, make signals and be handy at all the other endless chores required of a ship of war. The engineers, for example, had all been some kind of garage mechanics—any kind, most of them. Some of them learned quickly and became competent: others continued to be—garage mechanics. As a result, it was not an uncommon thing, at some inopportune moment, such as when a big liner in convoy was bearing directly down on you, to have your engines stop dead.

I remember this occurring once on a trip from Dunkerque to Dover, in one of the nastiest blows I ever encountered in the Straits. The engines just stopped: that was all. We began to slosh about, rolling so hard that one could not keep his feet. Some of the deck ammunition went overboard. I suppose we were in no very great danger, for we were extremely buoyant and could stand a sea that seemed to smother us, but conceivably, we could have been capsized. By and by, before that happened, the engines wheezed and started up and we went on our way again.

There came a dark night in the winter of 1918 that I shall long remember. All through the spring and summer of 1917, we had been encountering the all-too-visible evidences of the German submarines' prowess: between England and France, the sea had been almost literally covered at times with debris—furniture, bits of cargo, and saddest sights of all, that which had once been humanity. One day we came upon a lifeboat—empty! Another day—poetic justice—the thirstiest man in the fleet found a great hogshead of claret. He filled every utensil he had on board with the wine, down to his tooth glass, but the hogshead itself was too big for him to hoist aboard, so with a sigh, he had to cast it off still half-full.

Towards the end of 1917, we began to gain a little on the subs and by 1918, they were getting the worse of it. Our Dover patrol had a good deal to do with that. When I was first attached to it, the navy had already stretched between England and France, a great barrier of wire nets, with mines atached. As long as these could be kept in place, they were more or less effective in keeping the subs from using the Straits of Dover route to the Atlantic: by forcing them to go "north about" we made them add a couple of thousand miles to their routes out to the shipping lanes, and so, decreased their effectiveness.

But it was almost impossible to keep the nets in position. The tides sweep up and down the Straits with the speed of a mill-race, carrying everything before them except the most heavily moored of navigation marks. To string long lines of heavy nets from buoy to buoy was just an invitation to the tide to carry them away. Consequently the net barrage did not completely close the Straits.

Many other devices were tried. One of them, for example, consisted in extensive deep mine fields between Folkestone and Boulogne, with the top left free for surface craft. I helped survey the Straits for these mine fields in the summer of 1917. The idea here was that surface patrols would be so active and so numerous that the submarines would either have to try to fight their way through or submerging, hit the mines. I believe this had moderate success, though the joke used to go in the navy that there was nothing so safe as a British mine.

The next device—horribly expensive and elaborate—
was to surround these mine fields with a double row of
light-ships, anchored in position. At first, each of these
ships burned magnesium flares all night, so that the whole
sea from England and France was kept illuminated. Next
the flares were replaced by powerful searchlights, which
interlocked. There was thus a double route of lighted
sea-surface all the way from England to France. The
lighted lane was brighter than any city street. If a submarine came into the light, it was signalled and the patrol
craft in the area were supposed to deal with it. If it sub-
merged, it came to rest on the mines and presumably exploded them and itself. This arrangement was, I believe,
encouragingly successful, and the Germans had to send
most of their subs up around the north of Scotland before
they reached the open Atlantic. Merchant ship sinkings
fell correspondingly.

Naturally the enemy did not take this lying down. He
soon began to see that he would have to get his subs past
the light ships and the patrol vessels. The only way he
could do that was by breaking up the patrol lanes temporarily with surface craft and sneaking his subs through
on the surface while the action was going on. This he
attempted several times, and each occasion took the form
of a sharp and bloody naval action.

The general situation was as follows:

At the Belgian ports of Ostende and Zeebrugge, the
Germans had advanced bases for their submarines and a
number of their destroyers. Containing them, as the naval
expression is, were the various units of the Dover Patrol,
consisting in a score or more of destroyers, hundreds of
mine-sweeping and patrolling drifters, several large
paddle-wheel minesweepers (paddle-wheels to give them
shallow draft), a few big "monitors" with twelve and
even fifteen inch guns (used mainly for bombarding the
shore positions on the Belgian coast and in case the Ger-

man main fleet of heavy fighting ships should attempt to get through the Straits) and, among others, a large number of our small, comparatively fast "Motor Launches." Altogether, it was asserted at the time that there were something like four thousand ships attached to the Dover Patrol. I can believe it, for that dirty, dreary town was perpetually alive with sailors in their thousands.

An additional element of strength was furnished by the Harwich squadron of light cruisers and destroyers, for much of the war under the redoubtable Admiral Tyrwhitt. Harwich lies "just round the corner" from the Straits, that is, on the east coast of England, just north of the Thames.

Many of our Dover Patrol ships were based on the French port of Dunkerque. There usually lay there two or three monitors, a squadron of destroyers and numerous "M.L's."

This huge concentration of force was not merely a protection against submarines. Across the Straits, it must be remembered, went every man and every round of ammunition which the English-speaking peoples (with some American exceptions) were throwing into the fight against Germany. The Straits of Dover were the Allied jugular vein.

When I joined the Dover Patrol as a sub-lieutenant, I was appointed "First Officer" on Motor Launch 16. The chief function of this ship, one of the earlier models, seemed to be out of commission. By long odds the most boring period of my life was the long winter in dismal Dover during which old M.L. 16, was in a state of perpetual refit. I must say that British dockyard methods did nothing to hasten her back to life. Driven by sheer boredom and lack of any duties of importance, I got permission to hire myself out, as it were, to others of the Motor Launch fleet which for one reason or another found themselves short of an officer. This was the worst winter of the war, both by land and sea, and there began to be a good deal of doubt as whether the submarines would not triumph. To an impatient Canadian, whose instincts were all for doing something about it, the sang-froid and indifference of the British was often maddening. Every expression of concern at new losses simply seemed to be greeted in the same unvarying way: "Oh, it'll be all right. What'll you have to drink?" And here was I, just doing odd jobs, as it were.

By the summer of 1917, a more active spirit seemed to be coming over the Dover Patrol, and offensive measures began to be taken—not only the channel barrages which I have described, but daylight bombardments of the enemy positions on the Belgian coast and a rapid increase in day and night patrols. The change approximately coincided with the coming to Dover of a new Vice-Admiral Commanding, Sir Roger Keyes.

The Motor Launch patrols were caught up in all these new activities, and among other duties, we made night patrols along the Belgian coast off the ports of exit for the submarines from their shelters in the interior basins of the Belgian canals. Life ceased to be dull from that time on, for not only was there the novelty of French life to be encountered each time one went ashore, but there were also the daylight bombardments, in which we acted as the small pilot fish around the big shark bulks of the monitors, the long eery night patrols, and, just to keep the time from dragging, unending German air-raids by day and night.

The routine for our service was about three weeks in France, three weeks back on the English side, then a few days "standing by" and finally a few days "standing off." It was during one of the English tricks of duty that I encountered our friend Fritz for the first time face to face.

Our little ship had been assigned to a night patrol from the Folkestone "gate," where two light ships permitted an entrance to traffic through the mine fields, to the Varne shoal, and return. The Varne lies in mid-channel about half-way between Folkestone and Boulogne. Above it the water shoals to a few fathoms and the tides race over it hard. It was one of the anchors for the mine barrage.

We left Dover harbour at dark, proceeded westerly to the gate and shaped our course for the Varne shoal. Several hours passed uneventfully, the engines chugging along at low speed and the ship swinging round at each end of the line, to resume her course in the opposite direction. A sea patrol is just the same in nature and just as monotonous as that of the policeman on his beat. It becomes miserably cold up on deck—this was February—one walks incessantly up and down to keep awake and keep one's feet warm, there is little conversation, everyone is at the ready but no one is tense: it is routine work.

We went on like this for several hours. It was a clear, calm night, very dark, no sea. About midnight, a red Verry's light was seen, fired from somewhere off in the south. This was the signal for "submarine sighted." It was not our business to go off looking for submarines which did not come our way, but naturally our vigilance was heightened. About one a.m. firing broke out on the direction from which this signal had been made and we concluded that our patrol ships there were attacking. Suddenly and without warning, out of the blackness three destroyers bore down, steering south-southwest, right on the course for the firing. Now we knew that we had a destroyer patrol ready for action stationed in the Downs, which is the channel between the Goodwin Sands and the coast of Kent. The course of this patrol from the Downs to the point at which the signal was made would have been south-southwest and it would have led right by the spot where we then were. We were proceeding north-northeast, on the return leg of our patrol.

The destroyers were about one cable's length off, go-ing at tremendous speed, without lights, of course. Sud-denly, as they came abreast of us, they opened fire with everything they had. The sea boiled around us. We at once flashed our "recognition" lights, a secret combin-ation of red and green lights changed nightly. At that, they turned their searchlights on us, full blaze, and let us have all the more of it. Then suddenly they stopped. It was all over in a minute.

Anyone suddenly caught on a dark road in the glare of motor headlights will have a little idea of how we felt on board our little boat, but I don't think you can ex-tract the full total of eeriness out of a searchlight on land. It has to be at sea. There, with the abrupt change from pitch darkness to something like noonday, the slosh of the water, the gloom of the sea outside the pathway of light, the immense sensation of space, one gets its full value out of this sudden blast of light. I've had the experience when yachting, and it's startling enough then, under peaceful conditions, but when the searchlights mean business and tons of metal hurtle down the lighted path, it really does heighten the effect a bit. It made me feel like a very small mouse in a brilliantly lighted empty room, pursued by three large cats.

Fortunately we were on opposite courses and our total divergent speed was probably about fifty knots (say, for the landsman's benefit, about 58 miles). Within a matter of seconds, the destroyers had passed on. Everyone aboard put the situation together in the same logical pattern. (a) Our destroyers were off to engage the sub-marine previously signalled. (b) They had sighted us, not very far away and on the course. (c) At night, a low-lying motor launch looked quite a bit like a sub-marine running with little more than her conning tower exposed. (d) The destroyers had quite properly opened fire on us. (e) When we made our recognition signal, they put their lights on us, saw us and went on. (The firing had seemed to stop just after the search lights flashed.)

We picked ourselves up, as it were, and dusted ourselves off. All the ship's company was intact: that was the main thing. No one hit. A few stays dangled loosely from the mast. No other damage apparently—though by morning light we found a hole in the life boat, where a chunk of shell had torn through it.

But why had we not been sunk? That's what I asked myself at the time and what I have asked myself over the years, whenever the scene has flashed across my mind again. Destroyers in those days carried two guns forward, two aft. Three destroyers, twelve guns. Each of them about five-inch calibre. Various lesser weapons, equally deadly at short range. At a modest twelve rounds each a minute, kept up for, say, forty seconds, roughly one hundred major projectiles heaved at us. Distance, about one cable, 600 feet, about the length of a short city block. Logically we should have been blown to pieces, the ship and every man aboard.

Providential escape. Fortune of war. The destroyers had acted quite correctly in firing on us!

We continued our patrol. There were a few flashes more to the south, including one serious one, then everything quieted down, and we went back and forth uneventfully till dawn, when we came off patrol and made harbour. There we heard what had really occurred, and it was not much like what we had thought. The first submarine signal, we had got right enough. A small action had occurred and it was thought the submarine had been damaged. Then, as a considerable concentration of ships formed about the spot, some big paddle-wheel mine sweepers, included, firing was seen off to the north-north-west and suddenly three German destroyers appeared, letting go with everything they had. A number of drifters

were cut up. One paddle mine sweeper received a hit on a
depth charge, which exploded, cleaning out the after end
of the ship and inflicting a good many casualties. Other
light ships were hit and some were sunk.

So this was what had fired at us! It would have hurt
just as much to be hit by a British shell as by a German,
but somehow, the sense of fear which had inspired us
had been subtly different just because we had assumed
the firing had been in error. If the destroyers had not
been travelling at top speed in one direction—and ourselves in another—they would have got us for sure.

They got enough as it was. And they got back un-
scathed that time. It was not too difficult to pull off one
of these raids, for while our fast ships were constantly at
sea and imperceptibly accumulated more and more gear
which weighed them down and decreased their speed, the
Germans stripped their destroyers right down to fighting
weight for one night's run. That gave them several knots
more speed and allowed them to blaze away at everything
they encountered, in the certainty it was an enemy, and
get back before our destroyers could catch up to them.

The main purpose of the raids was plain. Sinking
the light shipping was useful but secondary. The point
was that under cover of the fight, with everyone's attention concentrated on the surface action, the enemy would
hope to slip two or three submarines through on the
surface, thus avoiding the dangers of the mines below.
He did this once or twice and then swift retribution
followed. One night submarines were signalled as before,
the intercepting destroyers dashed out as before, but this
time our destroyer patrol, that night consisting of the
Swift (with a six-inch gun, larger than anything the
Germans carried) and the *Broke* caught him, smashed
him up, sank several of his destroyers, actually "boarded"
one in old cutlass-in-teeth style, and captured ignom-
iniously several hundred of his sailors.

As we stood on Dover pier, during war time used as a boat landing, and watched these fellows, all looking very seedy and wet, brought ashore, we felt that things were evened up.

But what a part to play in the great game when it actually came! Stormed at with shot and shell, without ability to make anything more than a feeble catscratch in retaliation and genuinely convinced it was not a case for retaliation!

That's war.

Boredom, high moments, anticlimax.

XIV

Blocking in the German Submarines

THE night was dark and windless, the tide a few hours
from the flood. Far to the eastward an occasional uneasy
German searchlight pencilled the sky, and now and again
a chain of "flaming onions"—starshells—was thrown up
into the track of some real or imaginary allied airplane.
Here where I was, in the open roadstead of Dunkerque,
hundreds of ships were forming up into long lines,
arranging themselves in a predetermined order, carefully
nosing around each other, all without benefit of a light.
Outside, to seaward, lay the great monitors, with their
fifteen-inch guns—the *Terror,* the *Erebus, Marshall Sault,
General Wolfe,* and others. These great, slow ships were
floating gunplatforms of shallow draft, especially built
for shore bombardment work.

Closer-to stretched endless lines of sleek destroyers,
all lying low on the water, like dogs straining on leash.
And inside them again were the little "M.L.'s," the forty
ton Motor Launches on which I was serving. Eighteen
to twenty knots at maximum speed, and a little pop-gun
of a three-pounder gun: that was us. But there were
dozens of us and we had our own appointed tasks, not
unimportant tasks.

The scene was striking and in its way beautiful: the
low French coast: the dark waters: the infinite shadows
of ships. It was a battle piece and to the men about to go
into action, for the most part, I suppose, exhilarating.

If I may be permitted again to reminisce about that ancient war of mine—and various other millions of mankind—I'd like to talk about the way we blocked up the German submarines, cutting them off from the open sea, removing the pressure they had been putting on our merchant fleet, bringing closer the day when we'd force them to cry quits. That's what all this to-do was to which I've been alluding. After the Straits of Dover had been made difficult for submarines by the measures described in the previous sketch, it was necessary to finish the job and make them submarine proof. This could be done best by blocking up their lairs, the two ports of Ostende and Zeebrugge. These ports were connected by the Belgian canal system and it was thus possible for the Germans to send their submarines into the open sea through either of them. Both of them therefore had to be blocked.

The operation had evidently been projected as an integral part of the whole device for blocking the Straits, for rumours began to float round the Dover patrol not long after the light-ships had been put into position. These were vague but by the winter of 1918, the Motor Launch patrol at least knew that "an especially hazardous operation" was in contemplation. The small craft were put through fleet manoeuvres, something normally outside their province, and eventually, towards spring, volunteers were called for a "specially dangerous feat," nature not specified. Those were the days when the Germans were bending the Allies back day after day in the great March offensive. Every day it seemed as if Paris must once more fall and the Allied lines be broken. Perhaps it was an evacuation that was thought of as the "especially dangerous feat." No one knew. Many speculated that it would be some bold stroke designed to relieve the pressure on the military.

Eventually a certain amount of information had to be given even to unconsidered trifles like auxiliary patrol officers, so we began to understand something of what was up. Not until shortly before the blocking operations actually were carried out, however, was anything very specific revealed. At that we were not told much about the general nature of the operation but merely briefed on our own share in it.

The blocking operations of 1918 have been described by several previous writers, so there is no need to rehearse their details at this point: my object is simply to try to tell what they seemed like to one man on one small ship.

Early in 1918, the Motor Launches had been equipped with large cylindrical tanks, placed on the narrow passage ways which on either side led from the bridge to the after companionway. These passages were about eighteen inches wide and the tanks filled them: One had to step up on them and walk precariously along their rounded tops. They were filled with a sulphuric acid preparation which when expelled under pressure turned into a dense white smoke cloud: a Motor Launch scudding along "making smoke" from her twin tanks laid down a screen of fog which covered a wide area of sea. The mixture was villainous stuff that was always leaking out and burning the decks: a launch, already damaged in collision, was on one occasion set afire and burned up in this way. "Making smoke" added steeply to the already great vulnerability of our small ships.

The purpose of the smoke tanks originally had been to lay down smoke screens between the big monitors and their shore targets. Once these were down, the shore batteries could only fire back by taking sound angles or by airplane spotting. Smoke screens greatly decreased the risk of the offshore bombardments—for the monitors, if not for the smoke-makers! Now the same technique was to be applied to a much more ambitious operation, that of blocking the two ports. It became clear that one of the jobs to be given to the M.L.'s was to get in close and lay down a screen alongside the coast under cover of which the blockships could creep in, almost to harbour mouth, just making a dash at the last through the clear. With luck, the right force of onshore wind—in this case, north, would waft the smoke screen in along with them, giving them coverage all the way into the harbour mouth.

Most of the harbours along the north coast of France and Belgium are artificial: they are basins dredged out of the sand and entered through two long protecting piers. At Ostende, these piers projected several hundred feet beyond the short line and the distance between them was only about three hundred feet. At Zeebrugge, the entrance was sheltered by the famous scimitar-shaped mole, on which a great deal of tough fighting took place while the blocking operations were going on.

It was proposed to block both ports by sinking in each of these narrow fairways two old ships, ships previously filled with cargoes of assorted reinforced concrete. If the ships could be swung at right angles to the fairways and sunk in that position, they would act like stoppers in a bottle. Moreover, since no dredging then would be possible, the fairways would soon silt up. That this was no imaginary consequence, the slightest glance at a sandy coast on a windy day will prove. I remember when I first landed on the sandy north coast of France, some of the houses facing the sea, the sand not having been kept swept back day by day during the war, were practically buried.

To execute the operation proposed would call for the highest naval and navigating skill and for the happy conjunction of various natural phenomena. Anyone who knows the coast of the Pas de Calais and of Flanders knows how dangerous it is. The tides are rapid as mill-

races and sandbars numerous as streaks on a dirty wall.
In peacetime, these bars are all buoyed and lighted and
it's no great feat to pick your way between them. In
wartime, all navigation lights are out, most of the buoys
are removed, and the tides flow just as fiercely as before.
The chances of picking up in the dark on a bank are
decidedly good. Navigators must have all allowances
calculated in advance for set and drift by tidal currents,
must know the speed per hour to a fraction of a mile
and be able to prescribe a precise compass course. In
addition to which, as the historic rule of the road
directions bid, the sailor must

> Both in safety and in doubt
> Always keep a sharp look-out.

Natural phenomena include wind, sea, moonlight or
the absence thereof, time of high and low water, whether
tides are spring or neap. Here are five main variables to be
co-ordinated. In our case, we had to have the tide within
a couple of hours of high water either way, if the ships
were to be sure of getting into the harbour channels. Not
only that: we had to do it pretty close to "springs," that
is to the high high tides which occur only once a month,
when sun and moon are pulling together. Wind had to
be moderate, not a gale or there would be too much sea,
and it had to be somewhere from northwest to northeast,
otherwise our smoke would only be blown back in our
faces. The moon, preferably, should not be too much in
evidence, although we required her to be full in order
to provide us with spring tides. This was quite a large bill
of goods to demand from mother nature, especially at the
south end of the robustious North Sea.

The hand of God and those of the experts pointed to
the month of April, 1918, as the destined period. Tides
would be at springs about the 11th and, again, a lesser

summit would be reached about April 23. The moon should be behaving itself. The weather, as always, was unpredictable.

"Making smoke" was to be the job of the M.L.'s. But there was one much more dangerous mission for which they were suitable, and to this certain selected craft were assigned, a call having first been made for volunteers. The essence of the operations was to get the blockships into the two harbours, turn them at right angles to the jetty walls, sink them by flooding or other means and then get away—if anyone was left to get away! Some of the M.L.'s —one attending each block ship—were to be the "get-away" boats. They were to trail the blockships in, stand by while they were sunk, then take off the crews. Since each of the two long arms of both harbours—just like two sides of a street—was crammed with every species of weapon, large and small, the chances of any one coming out alive were not rosy.

My skipper at the time was a British Columbian of Irish birth, one of the fighting, Norman Irish. He had been forced to pass most of the war on peaceful beats far from action and now, transferred the "hot shop" of the Dover patrol, was enjoying himself immensely, although so far, nothing more exciting than air raids had come his way. Now, with the "opportunity" of the blocking operations presenting itself, he was determined to be in the thick of them. I agreed to go with him if selected. We were not selected. This angered my skipper greatly, and he began to spend a good deal of time badgering the Commander of the Motor Launch flotilla. The latter, a London timber merchant turned sailor, everybody agreed, was a rather fussy old ass, but I suppose his judgment was good in this matter, for without a pair of very thick glasses, the fighting Irishman was practically blind.

Eventually the Commander's resistance was broken and we were designated not rescue-ship but "stand-by boat," that is spare. The Dunkerque flotilla, of which we were at the time a unit, had as its duty, blocking the port of Ostende. The Zeebrugge operation was to be conducted direct from Dover.

The entire fleet waited day after day for wind and tide to come right. The tide was inevitable, but the wind was obstinate. At last, April 11, a signal was made: all ships to put to sea and take formation. It looked as if we were going to be merely one in a long line of fog-belching M.L.'s. At the last moment, just as the whole vast armada was about to move off, another M.L. came alongside and on it was the Commander: his own craft had broken down and ours was to take its place. This was all very well, but neither of us had quite bargained for being a rescue ship with old so-and-so himself running the show. Brave man he might be, but not exactly the kind of personality one wanted to wave once more into the breach.

The night was pitch dark and inclined to be rainy. There was scarcely any wind, but what there was was favourable. We passed the last of the blacked-out navigation buoys on our side of "the line"—that is, the projection seaward of the battle lines ashore, and plunged into the no man's land that lay off the harbour mouth of Ostende. Our objective was the "Stroom Bank," a sand-bank marked by a buoy. From that point a course would be laid to the harbour mouth a short distance away. Similar columns of ships were converging on Zeebrugge.

We hit the buoy exactly. Then defiling to port and starboard the M.L.'s began to lay down their smoke screen. Our own craft, M.L. 276, cruised about just at that spot. When the blockships came along, she would fall in behind them and follow them into the harbour.

The range on the buoy was so short and its position so definite that I made sure we were in for a bad time of it. Star shells were already lighting the sky and as soon as the noise of ships' engines was heard, heavy stuff began to come out our way. But the smoke screen prevented their actually sighting us and they could only conjecture what was going on behind it: no radar in those days. So it was just sporadic shelling and not a single ship received a hit.

But where were the blockships, the ancient cruisers *Sirius* and *Brilliant*, which had been scheduled to appear on the appointed hour, on the tick? We waited, and cruised, turned and cruised, waited and turned. No block-ships. If we had missed them, brave men might have died in the harbour because of our negligence. And it would not have been too hard to miss them in that dark and fog.

It began to grow light. Still no block ships. To be sighted in that position would have meant destruction, and to no purpose. The hour for withdrawal had long since passed. Order was given to shape course for home.

Arrived Dunkerque, a ridiculous little incident provided a touch of comic relief. The Commander was leaving us. Our ship lay under the huge quai wall there, the top of which could just be gained by standing on the top wire cable of what we courteously called our "bulwarks." This cable was slack and swung about. One had to step up on to it, grab the ship's mooring lines and then heave himself up on to the quai side. The Commander put out his hand. In my colonial innocence —I was a colonial then—I thought he was putting it out for the usual purpose, shaking hands all round on the conclusion of a rather trying night. I took it and murmured something like "Good-bye, Sir, better luck next time," but he said, slightly embarrassed, "Oh, I was not intending *that:* I wanted you to give me a hand up on to the quai." So proper impersonality had been restored.

After we had disembarked our Commander, the mystery was explained: in good military fashion which always involves at least one last-moment postponement (in my limited experience, one of the chief functions of the higher command is to postpone), the operation had been given a hoist. There had been no block ships, no support to seaward, nothing but long lines of M.L.'s, all furiously making smoke!

The worst of it was that now the show was probably given away, and we could hope for a hot reception next time. To offset this situation, a deep and cunning manoeuvre was devised: we were all to go out again in a night or two and batter away at the German positions from another angle. This would, it was assumed throw the enemy off the scent. His foes might be up to something, but to what?

We duly battered. The position of 276 was right under the guns of *The Terror,* laying down a screen between her and the shore. I remember at one point turning towards her. Just as I did so, she fired. I got the full glare of her two fifteen inch guns full in the eyes. The German coastal batteries got our range in seconds and the sea splashed around us much as in the night when the destroyers nearly got us. But again, not a hit, not a man wounded!

After the feint, north winds. Gales, in fact. A north wind sweeping down the length of the North Sea, into the shoal ridden waters of Flanders, is not to be trifled with. If anything goes wrong, you are on the beach in no time, which, during war, meant capture. So things just had to wait. At last, conditions coming favourable: wind dying, tide at medium springs during the graveyard watch; promise of a little moon, not too much. So April 23, was posted as THE DAY; St. George's Day, Shakespeare's birthday, it was, by happy coincidence, for those who speak the tongue that Shakespeare spake, and now, a generation on, it lives again, Zeebrugge Day.

My indomitably heroic skipper and pal—a dear, old soul he was, and I may as well name him, Roland Burke of Nelson and Esquimault—was determined to be in the thick of it this time, so he once more laid seige to the Commander of the Motor Launch flotilla. The blood of all the Burkes demanded the place of honour—for which, to tell the truth, competition was not overwhelmingly impressive—and the place of honour he at last got. But I was not to share it with him, for two days before, I had been given command of a little ship of my own—M.L. 274 (what a pity it is these little fellows were not named, for numbers are such impersonal things, and a ship is a personality).

In command of one of H.M.'s Ships of War. A pretty proud position for a young man. Pretty proud for us "colonials" who had, as it were, just "busted into" the Royal Navy. Well times have changed, but I still don't know anywhere else that I'd prefer to be rather than on the bridge of my own ship—that is, if I had a ship. I remained in command for a year, until I left the service to come home, and a good year it was. It fed one's ego a bit to hear men from other ships sing out for "your captain." I had never thought I would in my career be captain of a ship of war, for small as she was, she was still a sea-going ship, and her destinies and those of her men were in my keeping.

As a junior officer-in-command, I was relegated to the rank and file, and put in the column of smoke-making ships. This duty was not without its interest but it could not compare with the rescue work. All I had to do was to follow the ship ahead and see that my tanks were spewing out fog. On one occasion the tanks ahead failed, leaving a gap in the line: we just went on and the other fell back into our position until her tanks were got going again. Each time we would come to the end of our patrol, we would pop out of the fog bank for a moment to keep the screen extending. This was the enemy's opportunity. He could see the edge of the screen quite well, so simply ranged on it and let go. His fire was dense enough all along the screen, though it was all guess work, or barrage fire and not concentrated enough to do much harm, but at the edges it was really hot. Again, however, luck was with everyone and no casualties occurred.

It was an exciting night. Little wind, moderately dark, the sky pierced by the rain of German star shells, which redoubled once our forces were discovered. The roar of the shore batteries, the deep thunder of the monitors to seaward as their great shells passed overhead, the flashes of every colour tone and in every direction, made a battle piece just dangerous enough to lift the spirits, not horrible enough to slug them into terror.

During the night we saw the block ships go by. Good luck to them! Shortly after, to our horror, the wind shifted, a light breeze coming off shore. This rolled back our fog upon ourselves and left the block ships bare. Well, hard luck to them, but they had to do their duty as we ours, and over luck, there could be no repining.

Promptly at the scheduled hour, the recall signal was given and course was shaped for Dunkerque. Broad daylight when we made fast. All hands turned in at once.

I was awakened by my ex-C.O.'s voice bawling down into the cabin. His pet name for me had become "B.N.O." "N.O." is navalese for "Number One," that is, first officer. "B." stood for "Bloody." He was of too fine a fibre to go about singing out at me as his "Bloody Number One," so he compromised on "B.N.O." which became, I think, a term of endearment.

"Ha, ha, B.N.O.," I heard, "thirty-five survivors! *Thirty*-five survivors!"

Burke had in fact, picked up the entire crew of the *Brilliant*. The men he rescued had cheered him as they landed. Shortly afterward he was promoted lieutenant-commander and given the D.S.O.

Another close friend of mine, also from British Columbia, had been first officer on the M.L., which rescued the fifty men on *Sirius*. All the inshore work had been done without a smoke screen, but miraculously there had been no casualties.

Then came the dénouement. Air photographs showed that Zeebrugge, where landing parties had got up on to the mole and engaged the enemy at first hand with great gallantry, had been pretty well blocked up, but at Ostende —oh, ridiculous anticlimax—both ships were piled up on the beach half a mile away from the harbour mouth! That was probably the explanation of why there had been no casualties. No German in his senses could have imagined his enemy deliberately running his ships ashore to no purpose, so consequently since they should not have been where they were, they had not been. Little direct firing on them, in consequence.

The cause of the mischance came out later. Just the night before the attempt, the Germans, for reasons best known to themselves, moved the Stroombank buoy half a mile to the eastward. To the navigators on the block ships, a buoy was a buoy, to be sought and taken as guide. There was no other mark for the harbour mouth, anyway. So both piled up.

In view of the brilliant achievements of the Dover flotillas, the Dunkerque ships felt pretty low after this. It was therefore good news to hear that still another try was to be made. The ship which had carried the boarding party to Zeebrugge, the *Vindictive,* had been pretty badly mauled, so it was decided to use her as the next block ship. In full view of the public, she was filled up with the gravel from Dover beach, but despite this, the Germans did not find out what was going on.

Once more my former captain insisted on being on the rescue party. I think he must have carried his badgering of the Commander, M.L.'s, almost to the point of insubordination, though now that he was a two and a half ringer and a D.S.O., he could take a little more liberty than as a humble lieutenant. Anyway, his importunities succeeded. My own boat was once more to be a mere smoke-maker, with an exception. Finding the harbour this time was not to depend on perambulating buoys. The harbour was to be found, beyond the peradventure of a doubt. This job was assigned to the "C.M.B.'s," the Coastal Motor Boats. These were very fast launches, something like those that dash around Canadian summer resorts standing on their tails. They were low in the water, hard to hit, and would do about forty knots. They were originally designed for fast hit-and-run attacks, with torpedo, on surface ships. The point that interested me in this matter was that if the sea were too heavy for the C.M.B.'s or if for any other reason they could not operate, their job of finding the harbour was to be turned over to me. Along with another launch, I was to find the pierheads and then we were each to station ourselves just off them, to mark the entrance. Since the Germans undoubtedly had some quite healthy armament on the pierheads, this might be glory but it would not be fun. As it turned out, I just did my ordinary smoke job, as the weather was suitable and the C.M.B.'s found the entrance without difficulty.

On the night of May 10, the flotilla at the appointed time got to its rendezvous off Ostende, and smoke making began, as before. The night was perfect, the wind exactly right, all conditions ideal. Far to seaward, the huge guns of the monitors lit up the sky as they engaged the shore batteries, which replied in kind. Above, the air hummed with our bombing planes, and just outside us, the destroyers loosed off over our heads. Old Fritz responded with his usual display of star shells and flaming onions, along with everything else he had, but the smoke was so good that he could do no harm. One of the star shells fell right on the deck of one of our M.L.'s, but though it bathed everything and everybody on board in a strange phosphorescent glow, it did no harm.

About 2 a.m., the *Vindictive* passed us, her shell-tattered funnels showing up weirdly against the soft white banks of smoke. We went on with our smoke patrol until the recall signal was made and then proceeded to our berth in Dunkerque. This time, the rescue ships had had no picnic. 276 came back with hardly a plank in her that was not gashed by pom-pom or machine gun (Have I reminded the reader that these floating tinder boxes were all built of wood—good, inflammable pine?). The first rescue ship took off the *Vindictive's* crew and turned for the sea again. Then Burke, thinking the task done, prepared to follow her. As he left the harbour, he thought he heard voices calling him. He went back but could see no one. The second time, he turned to go, but again the sound of voices seemed to come. He went back again, but could find no one, but the third time, the calls persisting, he found the men who were uttering them, an officer and two men floating in the water, all three wounded. Burke's own coxswain, standing within a few inches of him, was killed, and several other members of his crew. He himself was not touched. For this deed, he was given the V.C. It was never more fully deserved.

The Zeebrugge-Ostende actions cost us several M.L.'s sunk, all at Zeebrugge, and a number of casualties. They represented the climax of the war. With both harbours virtually unusable, we had got the subs pretty well bottled up. Destroyer raids were still possible, and always there were bombardments to be carried out by the monitors against the shore batteries. But while further offensive actions of a sweeping character were planned—including one that may well have been the ancestor of the Normandy landings of 1944, none were attempted. For the tide of battle was turning, the German was soon on the run and peace just over the horizon.

The Motor Launches started out as The Great Naval Joke, "Yankee Boxes of Tricks" and so on. They would "go to pieces when the first seas hit them." But we faced many seas and few of us were the worse for our experiences. Some of the little craft had some notches on their tomahawks, standing not for scalps but for submarines. It was true that one seldom had a meal at sea that sooner or later did not slide into his lap, but, smallest commissioned craft in a great navy, we sometimes had the satisfaction of knowing that the long, lank destroyers had to seek harbour almost as soon as we did. We grew used to having the waves wash us down from stem to stern and we lost our fear at running with gunwales under: we ran, in fact, in practically every position except with our decks where our keels should have been. The little toy boats toughened and roughened us and made men out of many who had not been men before. Boredom, yes, that's war, but action made up for it. I suppose these were my most formative days!

XV

A Stern and Rock Bound Coast

THERE surely cannot be many coasts more difficult than that of Nova Scotia. Its cliffs rise up forbidding and stern; it is fringed with reefs and, as often as not, covered with fog. Its assets are that its tidal currents are not strong, rarely more than a knot or two, and that it has plenty of small, snug harbours—if you can get into them.

I sailed out of Mahone Bay one summer on a good, staunch thirty-foot sloop, *The Jewel*. One of the things I liked about her was her manageability: at a touch of the tiller, she would swing round on her keel like a ballet dancer on her toes. Her cabin had six foot head-room, which was a boon to a person like me, who was always bumping his head. Her only fault was her engine, which, like all yacht auxiliaries, it seems, could be counted on to fail at critical moments. People will lavish affection on every square inch of a yacht and then instal an engine that should only be used as an anchor, deep beneath the surface of the sea.

Our headquarters was that delightful basin set among the hills and islands which is known as Prince's Inlet. From it, many was the circuit of the islands in the bay which I made in the *Jewel*. We used to run out and lie off the outer side of Tancook or go beyond to Ironbound, well out at sea. Or we would sail across the

116

Bay to Deep Cove, and amuse ourselves working the boat up its narrow intricacies to the head. Circumstances prevented my going far out to sea that summer, but I did manage, despite them, to make one trip to Halifax. Going up, the trip was uneventful. Coming back the sixty miles, I was put through my paces.

I had one young man with me, who was no sailor. Scouring Halifax, I also found another who was willing to make the trip back with me, for the fun of it. Meantime I had suggested to one of my colleagues, a former prairie boy, that he might like a day's outing. So early one morning we loosed out our sails on the Northwest Arm, with a crew of four aboard. This was just the sleeping capacity of the yacht—two forward, and two in the really spacious cabin.

We ran down the Arm towards the open sea, with no wind, and at the mouth were confronted by a wall of fog. We dropped anchor and waited. My colleague had just the day to spend with me, and was expecting me either to get him to Mahone Bay for the night, or into some other little harbour whence he might return by bus. We were therefore both anxious to get on. When the fog thinned out a bit, we nosed around the point and out to sea. It soon came in again, thicker than ever, so I took her close inshore and we got into the entrance to Herring Cove, where the fog had not penetrated. I had often walked over to the Cove from town but had never sailed to it before, so we decided to enter and have a look round. In that clear salt water it gave me an eery feeling to see the bottom coming up to meet me—we drew six feet—but I relied on my chart, which showed nine, and went ahead. You could spit across the entrance, so it was a tight fit.

My impressions of the Cove from seaward are three: the largest codfish I had ever seen (draped over a fisherman's shoulder, it looked just like the pictures we used to see of Scott's Emulsion), the village idiot, still left in medieval freedom and neglect, and strong fisher maidens swimming in a mixture of cold, salt water and fish guts. Maybe it's not like that today.

When we got outside again, it was a beautiful bright day as far as the headlands, but, beyond them, all was murky still. A wind was picking up from the south, which meant that the fog was likely to be blown closer in. We waited for a while and then, unable to resist the temptation of the wind, decided to have a try out into the fog and see what we could do. We were encouraged by the appearance of a good, big clear path, which gave visibility of two or three miles. This was adequate, but would it hold? We got out some distance off the coast. A tramp freighter came out of the harbour, passed us, and disappeared into the murk. I ran out into the steamer traffic lane on a starboard tack, then came about and headed for the shore. There was now no prospect of getting to Mahone Bay by nightfall, so my idea was to creep along and get into Ketch Harbour, if I could, to allow my colleague to go back home. I should explain that I had never been along that coast before and had no personal knowledge of what any of it looked like at close range. All I could do was to take compass courses and keep a sharp look-out. I thought I would be able to get close enough in to spot an entrance, even if the fog were thick. Between us and the entrance to Ketch Harbour, the chart showed various shoals. The entrance itself was another bottleneck, only about fifty yards wide, as accurately as I could measure my chart: in fact, the chart, which was of small scale, just showed a little blob for the whole harbour. Beyond the entrance, it showed the land running out a bit and then turning again to the westward. To seaward, off the point, were the first reefs of the great sheet of the Sambro Ledges, on which many a good ship has piled up as she tried to enter Halifax. Miss the mouth of the cove and we were into this mess of the Ledges.

It was probably insane. I should have turned back and taken my friend up the Northwest Arm again, taken him ingloriously home under the blessed engine. I did not. He, too, wanted to go on, so we cast in on the port tack. The Halifax lad took his place at the engine controls below: he was proving a genius with the miserable thing, and it was purring gently under his hands. The young Lunenburger, I placed up on the bow as look-out, my friend from inland at the tiller and myself conning her. "A man with a college education should be able to do anything," one who had one once said to me boastingly. If he is a prairie man, he apparently can, for this novice from Alberta took hold of her at once, and after he had had a little practice, I felt quite safe in leaving the tiller to him. I merely stood up in the cock-pit and motioned my hand to him, port or starboard, "a little, or a lot." The signal worked perfectly.

We ran in, under auxiliary and sail, trying to get bearings from the sound of the fog-horns that were now bellowing up and down the coast like fiends of hell. It was difficult to do, for they interfered with each other. However, I took a rough calculation of our speed from our point of departure and got in to what, from the fog-horns, sounded comparatively close to shore. I had a healthy respect for that shore. A few days before, we had been passing Rafuse Island in Mahone Bay, with a light wind and a long rolling, but by no means heavy, swell. As the swell struck the southwest end of the island, it shot up into geysers of water, many feet high. Woe betide the small boat that ever got caught with those hammer blows.

It was now late afternoon. We came about, and struck for the open sea again. We ran on until we reached a point at which I thought we could turn and fetch a course for the harbour mouth. Unfortunately, close to that course lay one of the dangerous reefs which lie off Chebucto Head. However, keeping a sharp look-out, we decided to try it: it would be our last chance before dark, and I was certainly not going to be any closer to that coast after dark than I could help.

When we had been running for what I judged the right length of time, I had the engine shut off and went on under sail alone. It might be said that this was depriving us of certainty in return for uncertainty, but I felt that the silence which sail gave us was worth more than the manoeuvreability which the engine conferred, especially such an engine as ours. With sails alone, we had a chance of hearing breakers as well as of seeing them.

What happened was that we saw them and heard them both at the same time. In complete silence we stood in the little ship forging capably ahead, every eye and ear rivetted forward of her course. Suddenly with anguish, undue, in his voice, our look-out bellowed "Breakers ahead" and at the same moment we saw them, right under our bow, throwing up masses of foam as they broke on the rocks. We came about at once, and stood out to sea again. It had been close enough, but the breakers had been dashing against a cliff, not over a reef, so we had seen the main shore and had presumably avoided the reef—unless it still lay in wait for us, if we had to take another turn outward. The coast was trending inward, apparently, or away from us on our starboard hand as we approached it, so that there was a fair assumption that we had not passed the entrance to the little harbour.

I told my friend that I would take one more cast out and in, and that then, if we did not find the harbour, we would strike for the open sea, and he would not get home when he had expected. Working out to the open in itself would be bad enough, for the northeast reefs of the Sambro ledges would be lying in our way, and we would have to work around them before we could get right out to sea. Moreover, small boats are rarely adequately equipped for continuous sailing day and night, and for every eventuality; in that blanket of fog, for example, we had no fog-horn, so that if we had been run down by a steamer, we would have little legal recourse against her. However, if it should prove necessary to put to sea for the night, I hoped to get into the main channel and then run out to the outer lightship, where I could make a course for Ironbound Island.

We ran out a bit, came about and nosed in again. It was now getting dark. We soon saw the cliffs again, turned and ran along them. I saw a shallow bay in which I thought it might just be possible to anchor and lie for the night. While I was taking a look at it, someone exclaimed, "What's that up ahead? Looks like a build . . . why, it's a lighthouse!"

It was, it was the light marking the entrance to Ketch Harbour!

We ran on in, letting go our hook right in the entrance because the chart showed hardly enough water at that stage of the tide for us to go on up into the harbour proper. We had just finished making all ship-shape when a "put-put" was heard, and a fisherman came into the entrance. He stopped.

"Aren't you coming up into the harbour?" he asked. I told him I didn't think there was water enough, but he assured me there was, so we went on.

"Where'd you come from?"

"Halifax."

"I heard an engine out there, going right for the shoals, 'That's bad luck to them,' I says."

"Well, we didn't hit them, anyway."

"You've often been in here before, I suppose."

"Never been within five miles of it before."

The fisherman was patently amazed. "Don't know how you ever got in here in this fog," he said.

"Neither do I," I added.

Secretly, I puffed out my chest. Not such bad navigation after all, for an amateur. Did anyone say anything about finding a black cat on a dark night?

XVI

Down the Lakes on a Grain Freighter

FORT WILLIAM dripped with rain. The columnar tubes of the elevators shone sourly with it. The lean poplars showed no sign of leaf. From the ends of streets Thunder Bay loomed up sulkily. Mid-May, but not much of a day to be setting out off over those cold, northern waters.

Just beyond the elevators, a huge, red wall was discernible. This was the grain freighter on which I was to go down the length of the lakes. I went aboard, and was greeted, not as the interloper I was, but as the prodigal son returning. "We have a spare cabin up under the bridge," said the chief engineer, who hailed from Midland. "It's never been used yet—never had a passenger before. The pipes was all froze up with rust. You won't mind, I guess." I said the water would probably run clear in due course, and went to the "spare cabin." It was surprisingly large for a ship, and with a real bed in it. There was running hot water (rusty) and a shower bath.

I shared with the captain living quarters in that lonely house which sits up forward, right over the noses of the grain ships. He was a man fitted out for use, not appearance: that is, he wore no uniform but was an expert at his job. "You won't find it very interesting I'm afraid," he said, "we have to make calls at half a dozen elevators before we get under way. That will take most of the

123

night." I watched him nose his ship in beside one or two
of the elevators, and marvelled at the skill with which,
in the pitch darkness, he laid her six hundred feet of steel
alongside the quay: she came in as gently as a leaf falling.
That was surely interest enough, for one night.

In the morning we were out upon Superior, well past
Passage Island, with nothing in sight. It was a beautiful
blue and white day. I went aft for breakfast, picking my
way along the great stretch of steel deck, past innumerable hatches, yawning chasms last night, now all battened
down, and with a different parcel of grain for a different
consignee under each. I had conceived a grain cargo as
just half a million bushels poured right in. I found, instead, a complex of different wheats for different firms,
all kept securely apart.

In the after quarters of the ship there were two messes,
and, in another saloon, across a corridor, a table set in
state for one. That was for me, the passenger. "Do I
have to eat all by myself?" I asked. The steward was
visibly relieved. I could eat with the ship's company, and
"side" would be dispensed with. The steward was from
Parry Sound, as was the captain. The first mate came
from Collingwood and the second, who was the son of the
steward, was living in Port Colborne. The term "ship's
company" was here no misnomer: everyone came from
"round the lakes," they all had been sailing from child-
hood, and they knew each other like brothers—which is
approximately the way they conducted themselves towards each other.

The second night out, I had just got nicely off to sleep
when I was awakened by voices near my door: somebody
evidently was in trouble. I got up and came upon an
extraordinary spectacle. Sitting down was the second
mate. A slight, bald figure was weaving about him in a
night shirt: from the bottom of the night shirt protruded
two unimpressive bare, male legs. A third party stood

by, with a pair of pliers in his hand. With some difficulty, under the night shirt, I discerned the captain. "Willie was doing some chipping" (cutting off old paint and rust) "around that deck lamp for'ard," the captain explained, "and got a chunk of iron in his eye: could you help us get it out?" The third party, the chief, looked on helpfully, but engineers' tools are not the best for eye operations. I suggested a magnet might attract the splinter. They tried this and it worked. My stock went up. The captain went back to bed, his dignity, despite the night shirt, in no degree impaired.

Before turning in, I went out and took a look at the night. The northern sky was bright and clear, a suggestion of the aurora flickering in it; the sea, black! I suppose I may use the term "sea." Superior is impressive at all times, never more so than at midnight. But it is not the ocean, and on a clear night, ships are not long out of sight of lights. When I got up the next morning, we had just passed Caribou Island. We watched a small ship coming down from under it. The company to which "we" belonged apparently thought binoculars a luxury for there were none aboard to look at her through. Perhaps they were not needed: most of the men on the bridge seemed able to see just as well without them.

We threaded our way through the St. Mary's River and out into Lake Huron. Towards evening, I strolled past the chief's cabin. He beckoned me in. The captain was sitting there. Each of them wore a slightly conspiratorial air. "Do you . . . would you care to . . . would you have . . . ?" queried the chief?

"Yes, I do . . ." I said, coming to his aid.

"Would you like some water in it?" "Yes, please." We sat and talked. I dallied. The other two had consumed their portion with one single deft turn of the wrist. The captain looked at me curiously. "You sup that stuff?" he remarked. "Yes," I admitted, "I sup it." "Me, I can't sup it. Get her down and get her workin', that's my motto," he observed.

As we passed Detroit, a small boat lying in the stream came alongside. Someone lowered a bucket. It came up with the daily papers. In the Detroit river, where traffic is as heavy as on a city street, we could have thrown those papers aboard many a ship as we passed. Our captain's course did not suit one Yankee skipper, who came out of his wheel-house and roared at us angrily as we passed. The captain's only reaction was to remark that "those fellows have it a good deal easier than us: three mates aboard, eight hours each." "You go up light," I put in, by way of suggesting an explanation. "Usually," he replied, "they can always get coal up. Then, there's the autos." A passing ship illustrated his point. Her decks were covered with new cars: I counted over seventy. "That's just pure velvet to them," said the captain.

Out in Lake Erie, the string of small islands off Point Pelee came in sight, the southernmost point of Canada. It was high spring here. But the islands lie six degrees of latitude south of Fort William, remember. Our course between them lay just on the Canadian edge of the border. Some miles off, one could see the huge monument that the Americans erected to commemorate their victory of Put-in Bay, near which, in 1813, Commodore Perry defeated the British naval forces on Lake Erie.

Later on in the course of the trip, Queenston Heights with General Brock on top of it, came into view. This competition in international monuments, each higher and in worse taste than the preceding is now fortunately over.

As we approached Port Colborne for the run through the Welland canal, the second mate began to show new signs of life. This was home. "There must be plenty of work in the big factory there," I said to him, as we came in between the piers. "Not for Canadians (or was it "white men"?), he replied. "They're all foreigners: the ordinary man hasn't a chance, unless he's in right with the foreman, and he's not likely to be, unless he speaks their language . . ." This was turning the tables with a vengeance.

Old William Hamilton Merritt dug the first Welland out of the Escarpment, near Thorold, with pick and shovel: nowadays, the great freighters march down the mountainside on a giant staircase, through the great locks of the new canal. Thorold itself is "a city set upon a hill," its lights visible at night for miles over the countryside to the north. Its streets bear some resemblance to those of distant Fort William in that on them "old" and "new" Canadians mingle, but whereas in Fort William, all are a matter of yesterday, the old Canada of the Loyalist days still shines through in Thorold, fighting submergence in the new industrialism.

As the ship enters the huge locks and the ninety foot gates close behind her, the skipper calls down to the chief, "Please give us a good slow." "Hardest thing in the world," he says, turning to me, "to get a good slow." What he wanted was a scarcely perceptible, but steady, motion on the ship. A few feet error and her ten thousand tons would have made mincemeat of the great gates below her, of the canal and of herself. The skipper had heavy responsibilities: no wonder that he wanted "a good slow," with his ship in perfect control. And how he could control it! He took up his position in the lock with the accuracy of a man parking a car—with far more accuracy, indeed, than most drivers display.

So we passed out to Lake Ontario, free of the river, off for Kingston. It was now dark, and when the morning came, we were somewhere off Port Hope, to judge from the high ridge visible in behind the shore a few miles. At noon we were passing the Outer Ducks and an hour or two later, the grain elevator at Cataraqui Bay came in sight. "Hello, there's someone in there!" exclaimed the skipper in surprise. An interloper, apparently; a ship not belonging to the line.

"I think we'll lie here until we see what he's going to do," said the skipper, "You don't mind, I hope"—turning to me. "Oh, not at all," I said, somewhat bowled over by having the giant underneath us thus by inference put at my disposal. "At least," I went on, recovering my control of the situation, "not as long as I get ashore in time to catch the Ottawa train."

This was promised, and down went the hook. An hour or two later, we got under way and again the miracle of seamanship occurred. The interloper had left just enough room for us to squeeze in between his bow and the head of the quay. On we went, under "a good slow," our bow passing his by inches but never touching. Then as our stern swung opposite his bow, the engine room telegraphs clicked, the "good slow" became "astern," the propeller began to revolve anti-clockwise, throwing the cumbrous length of the ship over to port (which for the benefit of the landlubbers, means to the left) and against the jetty wall. We took up our position as exactly as a key in a lock. She came in within inches of her marks, and the hawsers were out and fast before one knew it was done.

It was all very ordinary to the ordinary men on board, all in the day's work. Yet there are other times. One of them came when, years later, the same chief engineer, sailing on another ship, felt her strike in the darkness. "When I felt her bump," he said, "I went down into the engine room. The engines were racing, so I knew we had lost our screw. The engine room was already beginning to fill, but I stood by for orders from the bridge."

He stood by for orders from the bridge while his ship was sinking. That was proof, if proof were needed, that

just behind the good comradeship and quiet efficiency
everywhere apparent on an uneventful trip down the
lakes, stand courage and a high sense of duty. Yet to few
is it revealed that as our Canadian wheat streams out to
hungry Europe, it is speeded on its way by men who are,
when emergency comes, "faithful unto death."

XVII

Mountain and Sea

I BEWAIL my inland birth and the fate that has cast my lot far from salt water. Ontario, my native Province, is fair, and its inland seas are passable imitations of the real thing. But they are not the real thing. Ontario's wilderness is deep and in selected spots, it adorns itself with a great beauty: the wide stretches of Lake Nipigon, for example, give to the low mountains about it a setting surpassed in few inland countries. For the superlative, however, one has to go further than the Nipigon: he has to cross the continent and gaze at that overpowering combination of sea and mountain which smites down the traveller as his train rolls into Vancouver. Wherever he may go upon the Pacific coast thereafter, that combination doubles and redoubles upon him its aesthetic blows.

The primitive we have with us everywhere in Canada, but not everywhere the majestic primitive. On our Pacific coast we are in the presence of the most majestic and the mightiest of the primitives, the transcendant primitives, which fill man's past and which his future will never obliterate, the mountains and the sea. They call to men with irresistible voice, as they have always called. I don't like to quote, especially sententiously, but I can't forget my Wordsworth at this point:

> Two voices are there: one is of the sea
> And one is of the mountains. Each a mighty voice . . .
> They are thy chosen music, Liberty . . .

I hope they will prove to be for us the chosen music of liberty: we need those strains in Canada. But whether they will always call out the spirit of liberty in the people who dwell among them, we cannot yet tell. We can, however, already be sure that they will stamp their seal on chosen spirits. Faced with crowded cities and the tyrannies that may arise in them, men will always be found who will lift their eyes to the hills, whither their legs will carry them. There will always also be men whose gaze is drawn out to sea, men who will get into their boats and strike out for new worlds, as have their fore-bears ceaselessly over the centuries.

The casual traveller will be half-blinded with his first look at those mountains and that sea, as one who takes a swift glance at the sun, but he may never get much beyond these first vivid impressions. If he is of a nature not much impressed by physical surroundings, he may, after a few days, cease to see either mountain or sea. In any case, first impressions will both be reinforced and in some measure, toned down with custom, as he finds out new places. But unless he is drawn into it and close to it, he will never capture the spirit and genius of the coast for himself. The best way of accomplishing that, perhaps the only way, is to go and see it intimately from a small boat. A steamer will not do: she is too remote, and her pace too swift. One must take to the sea for himself, poke into the heads of the inlets, go ashore and see the people, climb up the mountain paths, and, returning to his boat again, get far enough off the land to take in the sweep of it, the play of light and shadow over it, its combination with the blue of the sea, its off-lying islands, and its dis-tant, aloof glaciers: yet not too far, as when in a ship, to lose all contact, to overlook the islets and the little houses of men, to forget the cruelties of the rocks, the sweep of the tides, or the depths of a mountain shore that make every anchorage a problem, and nearly all a danger.

It has been my good fortune to coast that mountainous shore which trends west and north from Vancouver, and under various conditions of sunshine and of storm. I cannot claim to have seen the western sea in its uttermost fury: indeed, I suspect the Gulf of Georgia is not capable of the uttermost fury, and I note that the toll it takes of men and boats, compared with its sister eastern coast, or with the great inland lakes, is low. But I have at least seen it shaking its mane, and I have seen it in rain as well as in sun. In all its moods, it is a coast to be loved.

My best memories of it derive from a trip of fifty miles or so down from Pender Harbour to Vancouver. I had a little twenty-six foot cutter, which was stout and tidy enough except in that by reason of her full-length keel, she was exceedingly difficult to bring about: one could run her up never so sharply into the wind, and let go his jib never so precisely but the result was all too often the same—she would hang there for a moment or two and then slowly fall off. Often the only way of getting her over on the opposite tack was to jibe her. She was equipped with the usual auxiliary engine, guaranteed to fail when needed most. I was alone.

Leaving Pender Harbour early in the morning, I had the promise of a fine warm day and a favourable west wind. I had to use my engine to cover the mile or two to the harbour mouth, but at that point I got a little wind, eased my sheets full out, and set a course dead before the wind . Coming out of the harbour, I had passed a tug having behind it one of the Pacific's interminable tows of giant logs. I came out the eastern passage and she came out the wider, or western, so that I was a mile or more ahead of her when we gained the open Gulf.

The wind soon dropped off to nothing. I was anxious to get down during the day as far as Gibson's Landing, at the entrance to Howe Sound: otherwise, I would have to spend the night upon the open coast, which for a person alone, and one who did not know local conditions, was not an overly cheerful prospect. A week or two before a southeaster had come shrieking down out of the mountains and had shown me what wind and sea could really do to small boats. It would seem simple to go on under power, but if I ran the auxiliary too much, it was liable to shake loose in its main bearings. So it was to be for emergency only.

The tug solved the problem for me by drawing up abreast. I hitched on behind the tow, leaving the sails flapping, and crawling along at a mile or so an hour. I took the opportunity to go below and get food, but I had not been long there before I felt a bump. Coming up, I found the wind had sprung up again and I was riding up on the tow of logs. I cast off and soon pulled ahead of the tug. Our courses diverged. She headed into Secret Cove, which lay two or three miles off to port. I searched the coast line for its entrance, but even with my glasses could not pick it out, so little did it show in the line off the cliffs, until the tug revealed it by disappearing into it. As she passed in, she seemed to be taking her raft with her right into the solid mountainside.

I stood on, under a pleasant west wind, with as blue a sky and as blue a sea as ever delighted the heart of man. The clearness of the air was unusual for the Pacific, where, things are more often bathed in a soft haze. I floated lazily through Welcome Passage and past the Franklin Islands. Out into the open again, I made for Mission Point, which lies on the Vancouver side of Sechelt Bay. This was my widest crossing, one of which small boats and tugs with tows are always a little nervous, for it is open to the whole expanse of the Gulf stretching away to the north and west, beyond Texada Island. There are no coves into which one may run and the open shore does not provide good holding ground. On the

west coast good holding ground—thick clay mud, into
which your anchor will bite—is rare: the Pacific world is
too new for that. The very Rockies themselves are just
youngsters, not more than a hundred million years old,
and sun, rain, ice and waves have not yet ground them
into that fine sticky clay which makes everything filthy
but rejoices the sailor when the flukes of his anchor bury
into it and his ship comes up hard and decisively to her
cable.

British Columbian mud seems thin and brittle; one
needs far more chain and heavier holding tackle then
elsewhere. And so deep are the coastal waters that often
this thin mud itself is far below the length of a small
boat's anchor chain. Hence a night at anchor on a lea
shore is not an experience to be sought; one might find
his boat lodged on the boulders of the beach by morning.

But who could worry on such a day and in such a
setting? I sailed across the open stretch at just the right
distance off to allow the coast to display itself to its full
advantage. Far astern, out beyond the Franklin Islands,
lay the high mountain peaks of Vancouver Island. One
solitary glacier-covered peak was catching the afternoon
sun. Nearer at hand, just under my lea, bench after bench
of the mountain side opened out. One could trace for
miles the road cut along its flanks, and the houses along
the road. The giant harvests of the lumberman were
only too obvious: his assault on poor old nature had
robbed the hills of square miles of their covering, leaving
the soil exposed and brown, waiting for the rains to
ravage it. Where trees still stood—and fortunately most
of the mountains were still treed—whether they were the
alders and maples of the low benches or the cedars and
spruces of the high, from five miles off all alike glowed
russet brown. This rich brown, suggesting dryness, into
which all greens changed at a few miles of distance, is the

dominant colour scheme of the British Columbia coast, one of the paradoxes of a region of heavy rainfall. When later, on my eastward journey I reached Manitoba, a region of light rainfall, prairie grass and trees, that province by contrast with the brownness of the early Autumn coast, seemed a livid, almost a poisonous, green.

As the sunset flush moved off the glacier, I came abreast of the next island group, the Trail Islands. There I thought of anchoring. But the good wind invited me to continue. At dusk I passed the White Islets, inhospitable rocks that they are, and made up past them to the land. I lay to for the night at Robert's Creek pier. How stern and solitary it seemed lying there, with the water sloshing round the piles, no lights except the distant glows of Vancouver and Nanaimo, and the great logs of the piers towering dark and menacing above my little boat. I was glad when morning came and I could resume. Another perfect day, wind and weather just right, so I ran quickly on, across the entrance of Howe Sound, to the islands between Barfleur Passage and Collingwood Channel. I had one spot in mind: one delicious, perfect spot. I had been there before, some years previously. Could I find it again? I could, and did. It was a little strait between two islands, out of the wind, out of the sea, with woods coming down all about to the tidemark, and water so clear that I could see my anchor lying on the bottom out from the bow. Its identity I will not reveal, for I keep it in reserve. Those who know the coast and their classics may find it for themselves, for has not Horace described it for them?

O fons Bandusia, clariore vitro!

"Oh, basin of Bandusia, clearer than crystal." Here in this Bandusian basin, I lay, first swimming, then basking in the warm sun, and lastly consuming shameful quantities of the oysters I had brought with me. Oysters!

They, too, I leave in their secret place, but who would bother with other food when he could live so richly on the sea's bounty?

After my feast, I weighed anchor (my inland tongue was on the point of making me say that I pulled up stakes) and made for the inevitable goal of Vancouver yachtsmen, Snug Cove on Bowen Island. You can be sure of Snug Cove's mud: when your hook is down, your boat will stay where you left it. Snug Cove, in other words, is snug.

Neither a hard nor an adventurous voyage, I must admit. But one sufficient to burn into the voyageur memories that will never fade, memories of colour and of form, of mountain and of sea, that will draw him back, I suppose, as they have drawn men from the beginning, as they will draw them to the end.

XVIII

Trans-Canada Crossing

I BEGAN my trans-Canada journey at the proper spot—
down in Cape Breton, where the Atlantic meets the Gulf
of St. Lawrence. The Province of Nova Scotia, with
commendable wisdom, has built a road around the beautiful northeastern peninsula of Cape Breton, which it calls
the Cabot Trail. The name is not quite as commendable
as the road, for John Cabot almost certainly did not make
his landfall on Cape Breton but on the east coast of
Newfoundland. Newfoundlanders now have a family
right to complain at another Province taking over their
John Cabot—and they do complain.

If you are ever in Cape Breton, go round the Trail:
you will see some of the finest views of mountain and
ocean to be encountered anywhere. And you will meet
a brand of Canadians who will probably be new to you—
the shy, proud Highlanders who still retain their Gaelic
and their reserve. They are polite, with an old-world
courtesy, meticulous in their duties as hosts—and aloof
and remote. The difference between the open-hearted,
gregarious Newfoundlanders and these austere, with-
drawn people is great: two very different breeds on either
side of Cabot Straits.

Back from the Trail, one should run through Sydney
and go on out to Louisbourg, the great French fortress
of the eighteenth century. There are people in the

modern town who will tell you just where Wolfe's men, hitching themselves to the guns, dragged them through the bush. They hitched themselves to the great guns and dragged them from the point of the landing till they got them into position to bombard the French batteries. The fort today is just a maze of stone ruins, though excellently taken care of. Apart from Quebec, Louisbourg is the most impressive historical site in Canada.

If you don't care for history, perhaps you like wild strawberries. If you have ever known a Maritimer, you will have heard all about the wild strawberries of the Maritimes. Louisbourg strawberries are tops: I wonder if that's because they grow in the graveyards—the old military graveyards. There are two of these, Catholic and Protestant. Either religion makes good strawberries.

All Cape Breton is beautiful. But much of it is abandoned, for it has not the beauty of utility. All Nova Scotia, indeed, is attractive—but much of the Province is wilderness. Yet a Province not too well endowed by nature keeps itself going from its own inner vitality. It is, one gathers, a supreme privilege to have been born in Nova Scotia. This *espirit de corps* means much: it means the effort to make the most of what you have.

Considerable contrast is afforded by the next Province, New Brunswick. Unpainted fence rails, other little indications by the way, point to a smaller fund of energy. The reason is plain: New Brunswick is not the close-knit community that Nova Scotia is: New Brunswick consists in two big halves, the Bay of Fundy section and the North Shore, and it is still further divided by its river valleys. Each valley tends to be a separate little world, not much interested in the Province as a whole—still less in the country.

The transcontinental route turns northward at the Isthmus of Chignecto and follows up the North Shore. One goes through the old lumber towns, with decaying groups of English in the big houses and thronging streets where the French live. Above Chatham, the road lies through country newly broken, where the French Acadians are at last rolling back the forest which the lumbermen managed to maintain for a century. It is strange to find a genuine "western" frontier of settlement almost in sight of the Atlantic.

Along the Matapedia, Acadia gives way to New France. English disappears. At least, not quite. We had a flat. The men in the service station were obliging but how could the anglais talk technical motor terms in French? The difficulty was soon solved. "Mettez le jack sous le roue," said one garage man to the other. That gave the clue. "Voici le valve," "ôtez le tube," that did the trick.

At Rimouski, out on the St. Lawrence again. We had begun at its beginning and now here we were, five hundred miles further inland, but with the great estuary still salt and so wide that no land could be seen across it. At Rivière du Loup, miles farther up, the river is *only* sixteen miles across. And then the colouring: Nowhere else have I ever seen such blues as in the water and islands of the lower St. Lawrence.

What attracts me most on that long stretch of the south shore are the 18th-century churches, with their fine symmetry and their interiors shining in gold leaf. Here is true Canadian architecture—almost the only architecture of any merit that we have. Upstream from Quebec, 18th-century taste in churches gives place to the garish monstrosities of a later day. Before the English Conquest, this little people, the French Canadians, possessed their own souls. For a century after it, they fought desperately to prevent themselves being ground up in the English mill. The next century—down to the present—they took up in regaining their self-confidence. Is it this self-assertion which the size and ostentation of their modern churches represents?

There is no mystery about what the older churches represent. Go into the church at Beaumont, near Quebec. There in the vestibule, seen by everyone every Sunday, is the order given by General Murray during the campaign of 1759. Let the inhabitants submit themselves to the protection of the King of England. Those who do not, will be taken prisoners and their houses and barns burned (as many of them were). The memory of that notice, in the interests of our common country, might better be buried, but the experiences it recalls are the stuff of which peoples are made. English-Canadians, with little but tales of pioneer bushwhacking to fall back on for their historical heroisms, will never understand their French fellow-citizens until they realize that this race has passed through deep waters.

From Quebec to Trois Rivières the north shore is the more interesting. We stopped for the night just west of the city, at some cabins on Lake St. Peter. I paid for our accommodation in bills of the Bank of Montreal—the old bills, which were in English only. "Have you any Canadian money?" the proprietress asked. I called her attention to the fact that they were Canadian. "Oh, I suppose they are—but they're English, you see," she replied. Montreal can be bypassed by cutting across from the foot of the island to come out on the Ottawa River at New Glasgow, where Sir Wilfrid Laurier spent his boyhood. New Glasgow is still an island of Scotland enclosed within French Canada. But most of the country of the lower Ottawa, once English in speech, is now French. French farmers occupy houses which from their build, must once have been in English hands. The French are in the houses, the English in the graveyards.

The road between Montreal and North Bay follows the old fur-trading route—up the Ottawa and across by the Mattawa to Lake Nipissing. Believe it or not, the fur-traders in their birch canoes used to cover this stretch in time that compares respectably with that of a modern motorist. There is a record of a trip from Sault Ste. Marie to Montreal in a week. A short generation ago this "back way" was in much the same state as in the fur traders' day. Today tourist facilities sprout everywhere. If one has an eye for country—which provides half the interest in travelling—he notes that the Kingmere range, feature of the view from the central square of Ottawa, runs along the north shore of the river, parallel to him as he drives. It gradually closes in to the shore and at Chalk River, where the new atomic town is, the great barrier of rock rises a thousand feet sheer from the river. Here it is a bold red in colour and its cliffs form the resting place of innumerable gulls and other birds. Hence its name, Bird Rock—Oiseaux Rock, or as they say it locally, "Weezy" Rock.

At "Weezy" Rock, the Ottawa is at its best—mile after mile of wide straight river, and deep in proportion to the height of its mountains. This stretch is appropriately called "Deep River": characteristic of the country, few Canadians know that it exists.

Deep River ends at the St. Joachim rapids now flooded out by a great hydro-electric development, but the rock barrier continues along the upper Ottawa to Mattawa. At Mattawa, which is the Ojibway word for "confluence," another river comes in from the west, and the road follows its valley to one of our minor Great lakes, Lake Nipissing.

From North Bay, on Lake Nipissing, the road swings north to Cochrane. Just a few miles out of the town, the familiar maples and elms disappear and the spruces, balsams and poplars take their place. Here begin the

"North Woods," as the Americans call the bush. In typical Canadian style, up here the province of Ontario has tucked away one of the best of its highways. The Province's main highway—No. 2, which nine out of ten American tourists travel on—is a disgrace and a danger. Nobody can accuse us of putting all our goods in the shop window.

The road west from Cochrane runs through what a generation ago was almost unbroken wilderness but today is comparatively well-settled country. In this "Clay Belt"country, you have crossed the great rock barrier between eastern and western Canada, the so-called Canadian Shield, and are coasting along on its northern edge. The Clay Belt may some day be a larger farming district than southern Ontario and Quebec. Virtually all the settlers are French Canadians.

West of Hearst, the Trans-Canada highway cuts back slightly to the south and enters the Canadian Shield again. For a hundred and fifty miles, there is neither house nor filling station. Then the "oases" of the mining settlements at Long Lac and Geraldton appear out of the bush and disappear into it again. After Geraldton, in country that a few years ago was as inaccessible as Central Africa, comes another "oasis," the little town of Beardmore. No one who did not know the bush as unbroken forest can have much of an idea of the thrill that these little settlements bring—opening up the bush is as revealing as the melting of the snow in the Spring.

A few miles before Beardmore the country changes. High bluffs, deep red in colour, take the place of the granite ridges. These signal Lake Nipigon, another of our minor "great lakes"—but a lake greater by far than any the United States or Europe possess, though as little known to most Canadians as the Caspian Sea.

Lake Nipigon is a lake with scenery and fish enough to stir the hearts of the dullest, but the only people

interested in it seem to be Americans: the unadventurous
Canadian rarely penetrates to these remote fastnesses. To
most of us Fort William and Port Arthur themselves
are only grain shipping ports. But as you stand looking
out over Thunder Bay, do you realize you have driven
over two thousand miles and are still on the waters of
the St. Lawrence—and still not half way across your
country? If by some unlikely chance you do, I venture to
say that you have never seen the beautiful country, some
of the most attractive in Canada, that lies between Fort
William and the American border.

Three hundred miles more of rock and muskeg, of
rivers and majestic lakes, three hundred miles more to
the west and you are out of the bush. The rocks of the
Shield sink lower and lower until, just a few miles east
of the little Manitoba town of Whitemouth, they disappear and the prairie stretches out in front. The road
becomes straight as a die. Three elms ahead give an
Ontario touch. Farms appear. A door opens into another
world.

And now a thousand miles of farm-land, straight
prairie roads, farm-houses behind their poplar wind-
breaks—but no barns—little towns at intervals, and everywhere the grain elevator. Winnipeg, Regina, Calgary, all
the familiar cities. To the easterner the plains look dry,
the trees small. But try reversing the process and come
on Manitoba from the west. Come on it from the treeless
plains, from the bald prairie. It then takes on the aspect
of a well-treed, verdant Province. And in winter its
poplar clumps standing up above the snow make its
countryside as beautiful as a great shining sea filled with
islands.

Near Regina the trees disappear; the bald prairie
engulfs one. The people of Regina have dammed a creek
and created a little lake in their city, where enthusiasts
far from the sea sail tiny yachts. When I first saw Regina,

back in the bad days of the drought, the lake had disappeared into a bed of mud. And going on west, one had to turn on the lights in the middle of the day, so dark did the dust storms make it. In the midst of one of them, I could see the outlines of a man ploughing. Poor fellow, every yard his tractor went, he was helping to destroy the very earth by which he lived. Houses were deserted, fences covered by the drifting soil. Saskatchewan in those days looked as if it had been under the foot of an invading army. Today recovery has come and the amount of permanent damage is said to be small. But drought lies just around the corner and much of Saskatchewan is always on the edge.

Travellers by train usually do not see western Saskatchewan and eastern Alberta, for the trains go through at night. If they were to see parts of them, they would think they were having a bad dream. Here on the borders of the two provinces lie the Canadian "bad lands," staring vistas of earth without life, weirdly coloured and threatening. "Could I have a drink?" I asked at a service station: "Well, be careful of the water: we haven't had rain here, to speak of, in three years," was the answer. I was glad when this country lay behind me.

At Medicine Hat, a little, blessed rain. First encounter with Alberta's natural gas. Medicine Hat has one claim to fame which is not advertised: here on the shores of the South Saskatchewan congregates in large numbers the innocent but not innocuous rattlesnake. A friend of mine told me that, going out in his garden one day, he was just in time to prevent his little offspring bending down and caressing one. Mishaps, however, appear rare.

At Tabor, wind. Then three silent peaks, far to the south, which marched with us as we drove, sentinels of things to come. At Lethbridge, still more wind; at MacLeod, more and more. A windy spot, this foothill region, with that great ice-box of mountainous glacier hung up above it. The road shoves on up and up to Pincher Creek, where they now have drill holes down more than two miles in search for oil, and with the crest reached, into the recesses of the Crow's Nest Pass. Here at Coleman, astride the continent, we are in the gloomy centre of one of Canada's major coal-producing areas. People of a dozen national origins have drifted there; prominent among them the Welsh. Welsh in the North Sydney coal mines and now Welsh again three thousand miles away on the continental divide.

Once past Coleman, the transcontinental voyager is in still another new world. In the middle of May there were six inches of snow in the Crow's Nest: a few miles further on, with the water running westward beside the road, the wild roses were in bloom. We found a shack with a stove in it on the mountain side, cut some wood and made a fire. What a joy to be in the forest once more! But what a mess man had made of the forest! Everywhere one went in British Columbia great sections of the mountain sides were covered, not with trees, but with stumps. British Columbia, one is sometimes inclined to think, consists mainly in stumps.

That night we camped in a wide meadow not far from Cranbrooke. To the west, a jagged peak glowed rose and violet in the setting sun!

My route was slightly unorthodox. I went from Cranbrooke to Creston, across the Kootenay Lake to Nelson, thence through Trail and Rossland to the Okanogan country at Penticton. On the way, one crosses three great ridges, with valleys dropping away beside the road for a thousand feet. On one stretch, the car ran twenty-seven miles in low and second gear. The down grades were frightening to the easterner but they seemed to hold little terror for the natives: at one particularly trying point, I was alarmed by a loud horn-blast from behind me and before I knew it a great wood-truck tore past at a furious rate, with two wheels hanging over the edge of nothing. "We go to sleep, driving on the prairies," a mountaineer said to me, "there's nothing to watch out for."

The westering sun was turning the waters at Ossoyous a dull blood-red as we began the four thousand foot descent from the last ridge, four thousand feet down something little better than a bush-trail. Nature seems to take care of its own in such situations: there was the Chinaman, for example, in the ancient Ford, accompanied by his seven children. He and his car slipped over the edge and rolled down several hundred feet. At the bottom, there was nothing left of the car, but the Chinaman and seven children picked themselves up unconcernedly and walked back up the hill.

The Okanogan with its pleasant little towns and its fruit ranches—everything is a ranch in B.C., even a patch of strawberries, which is a strawberry ranch—constitutes a good big stretch of settled countryside. Since fruit-growing seemed to offer an easy and profitable way of life (deceptively as it proved), it originally attracted huntin' and fishin' Englishmen. They built large houses and some of their private schools still flourish. Many of the grandees were starved out long ago, to be replaced by farmers who take their coats off, but a good number still remain, keeping themselves as aloof as possible from plain Canadians, fighting the losing fight to maintain caste distinctions on the edge of the wilderness.

The Okanogan country lies in a mountain trough. It is one of those valley settlements which make up interior British Columbia. Each of these valleys, the Okanogan, the Kootenay, the Arrow Lakes, Salmon Arm, the Fraser valley itself, has a distinct life of its own. To talk to people from all over British Columbia is to talk to individuals each with his own problems and his own special interests: there is nothing resembling the economic and psychological unity of the prairies.

At the northern exit from the Okanogan stands the town of Kamloops, on the banks of the North Thompson, that great tributary of the Fraser which does *not* water the surrounding country: the river just passes by and leaves the land dry as a bone. That is one of the shocks the traveller in British Columbia gets—the amount of desert there is. It all depends on which side of the valley you are: the eastern or lee sides of the mountains are dry, the western sides of the next range inland catch the rain and are covered with dense vegetation.

From Kamloops the road runs right down the valley to Vancouver. Between Lytton, where the North Thompson joins the Fraser, and Hope, some 70 miles, it crosses through the Coast range and begins to drop down to the Pacific. Here we are on historic ground. Through the great gorge of the Fraser, nearly a century and a half ago, went Simon Fraser, on his trail-blazing exploration to the Pacific. Anyone looking at the foaming water today could hardly imagine himself paddling down it in a canoe, but that is what Fraser did, and where he did not dare to risk the rapids, he scrambled along the cliffs: how he got through, it's hard to understand. Sixty years after Fraser, British engineers hacked out a wagon road from those very cliffs, the famous Cariboo Trail.

Going over the ridge and on down the slope to the Pacific is like slipping through Alice's looking-glass: the desert is left behind and one is in another world, the world of the great Pacific forests, the forests of three hundred foot trees. Even Fraser came down the river slowly and in daylight and the glories of the end of the trip came to his eyes gradually. The modern motorist does the same, but the more prosaic railway traveller has the better of both of them, for, projected through the darkness into this totally different and magnificent world of the Pacific, he wakes up in Vancouver, gets off his train, goes outside the station, and, if he is a person of any sensibility, rubs his eyes, hardly able to believe that what he sees is real—the great bulk of the mountains flung at him from across Burrard Inlet.

The best way to have this overwhelming experience of arriving at the Pacific is to make sure you get there on a bright sunshiny day in May, rush from the station into a taxi and drive out to Point Grey with your eyes shut. There, in the middle of the University campus, open them and behold all round you the sea: see the surf breaking on the rocks away over by the Point Atkinson lighthouse: see the distant mountains, softly glowing white, miles away beyond Howe Sound: see Vancouver Island forty miles across the gulf: and see, most of all, the great peaks across the harbour crowned with snow. The whole effect is breath-taking.

You will have to drive between four and five thousand miles and cross five time zones: you will have some bad road and some queer places to stop in, but if you will put a tent in the back of your car and imagine that you are Champlain, Radisson, La Vérendrye, Mackenzie, Fraser, all rolled into one, I think you will agree that one of the supreme experiences of your life is your Transcontinental journey. I wish you would take it. I guarantee it would make you a real Canadian.

XIX

Across the Atlantic with 1500 Highly Explosive Students

THIS TIME the ship lay not in Montreal but Quebec. And she was not a British merchantman carrying high-powered munitions but a big, solid old Dutch passenger vessel, the *Vollendam,* carrying equally high-powered American students—with a leaven of relatively staid responsible introversion from Canada. All were off to spend a summer in Europe, all straining at their leashes to get away into this new field of experience. Some of them turned up at the last moment in cars complete with leave-taking parents. The latter were promptly discarded. Most came under their own steam, and from all parts of the continent.

The ship was to sail at four p.m. The recall signal was made to the cafés of Quebec, whose personnel surely had never before come under such concentrated fire from text-book French. Passengers streamed in from every direction and after a long tiresome wait in the sheds, went aboard. Between students, baggage and sailors there hardly seemed a foot of space left on the decks; what there was was quite exhausted by the high velocity of the students, each one of whom, as soon as he got aboard, began to make his own continuous private voyage of exploration from bow to stern and back again to bow. However, we settled down at last and eventually got fed (that is the

149

right expression, I think). It became dark and the ship
was still at the dock. By morning, she was still at the
dock! Ship-breaking was then only prevented by threat
of instant departure.

Eventually we got away. The old ship had been an
army transport during the war. They told us she had
once carried six thousand men. Now she had less than
two thousand people, crew included. That would seem
to have argued plenty of room. It did not. It merely
meant that they had taken down the third tier of bunks
in the holds and no longer slept in relays.

Before we were out of the St. Lawrence, the usual
boat drills were held. This is ship's routine and I only
mention it because of a remark of the first officer. He
was instructing us how to adjust our life belts. One lady
insisted on wearing hers like a brassiere. He showed her
how to get it up under her chin and keep it there. "You
see," he said, "if you have to jump into the water"
(which was just a mere fifty feet or so from the boat
deck) "when you hit the surface, that belt worn like that
will spring up and break your neck." She, who looked
as if her shoes had never been off pavement, jumping
into the water and from a height of fifty feet! "It doesn't
matter," he added consolingly, "there are far more people
on board than we could get into the lifeboats anyway!"

Imagine this attitude of casualness on board the ships
sailing under the flag most often seen in the St. Lawrence!

Along with a few others I was a mere elder statesman
going along as guide and counsellor. Never were such
services less in demand. Young men and young women,
all had the air of being quite competent to look after
themselves, thank you.

At first I found myself down in the afterhold, along
with the boys. This was all right with me: I was an old
seafarer and comfortable enough on a narrow canvas
bunk. But the lads in the immediate neighbourhood were

a little embarrassed, I think, at having an old man with
them, and I suppose it was not quite compatible with the
dignity of age. So the competent secretary of our Canadian
party, Mr. Mathew Saunders, got me transferred to a
cabin of a dozen berths, where I was among the other
seniors. Only two of them have left any lasting impression
on me, both clergymen. One was a youngish Dutch pastor
who had come as chaplain with the immigrants the ship
had carried on her outward voyage, the other a German
Catholic priest. The priest was a meek little man, who
had emigrated to the United States at the end of the war
and now, four years later, was returning to visit his
native land. He was patently aghast at the complete
absence of tutelage for the young ladies, their appropria-
tion of whatever range of freedom and independence
they desired, and probably, as a European, misunder-
stood. The Protestant minister, reflecting the religious
situation in his native country, was rather aggressive in
his Protestantism. It was poetic justice which put them
in the same corner of the large cabin, one in the upper
berth, the other just under him. They had to make a
little conversation now and then, but I never noticed it
degenerating into cordiality.

I talked to the Dutch pastor about his immigrant
charges. They had been sorry to leave Holland, of course,
but, oh, so happy at the chance of getting to Canada.
"Lucky people!" he exclaimed feelingly.

After a day to settle down, a programme evolved.
This was no ordinary ship and no ordinary ship's company. There was a company of young Dutch student-
players aboard: their performances were splendid. Among
the Americans high seriousness was engagingly mixed
with exuberant frivolity. Consequently not only were
there the usual ship's entertainments such as dances and
so on, but also morning, afternoon and evening lectures.
There were lectures on history, there was sun-bathing,

there were lectures on philosophy, poker games, lectures
on art, petting (plenty of that), lessons in German, fancy
dress (or rather, undress) occasions, Student Christian
Society study groups, lessons in Spanish, folk-dancing,
weaving, French classes, church services, Republicans Re-
publicing, Communists communizing, lessons in Italian,
and each day a public meeting and forum (which, inci-
dentally, as a representative of our Canadian group and
as a Canadian I had the privilege of addressing). There
was, in short, everything. High pressure all round.

Our own group provided one of the ship's figures: a
professor of history going to a semi-religious conference
in Switzerland, whose chief business really was to observe
and report on the birds, the real birds, encountered in
passage. This gentleman was never seen without his
armament, which consisted in a pair of binoculars, high-
powered, of course, like the students. I understand he
made valuable observations on the presence far at sea of
wild life, feathered.

The phenomenon which chiefly intrigued me was the
difference that quickly manifested itself between the
Canadian and American students. There were about
seventy-five Canadians all told within the larger mass, of
whom about fifty were travelling as a party. This inner
group naturally came together at once and stayed together,
but the others soon adhered to it too, and cohesively.
The Canadians did not stick out like a sore thumb, but
they did stick together, both English and French, so much
so that some Americans began to notice it and to tell
them they were "clannish." Still, it was significant to see
the way English and French came together on a basis of
all-Canadian chumminess when in the presence of the
larger group.

The voyage, if it did nothing else for me, read me a
lesson in our own Canadian characteristics: our youths
were quieter, more retired, less exuberant than the

Americans. While the Americans, in general, seemed completely without inhibitions, our young people were restrained: their high spirits stayed within well-defined marks. The Canadian girls were, without exception, ladies.

Intellectually, the Canadian students were not as much interested in a wide bill of fare as the Americans (I would hesitate to say that this carried the implication "deep rather than wide"), not so emphatic in their discussion, less varied in their culture, which reflected faithfully their English and French origins and did not draw very much from the wide European world as the culture of many of the Americans did. Our students were more conventional, not so experimental, much better disciplined from within, did not have the high sense of intellectual adventure which many of the Americans seemed to possess. While equipped with much more emphatic norms of deportment than the Americans, they were not grounded in the same sure sense of themselves and their society. They were representatives of their people—solid citizens, capable, with plenty of controlled energy, good dependable men and women.

Naturally the differences between the youth of the two countries should not be overstressed. They are mostly those of social habit, social tone and pace. On the big political fundamentals, there is not much difference. For example: one morning a Dutch professor on board gave a lecture on Dutch law. In the course of it he observed that Holland, as a Roman law country, never had had the jury system. He went on to deprecate the jury as an institution. This provoked a storm, the American students without exception championing the jury system. The incident contributed a good illustration of English traditional institutions held in common.

After we got clear of the Banks and the sun came out, the full blast of unconventionality unleashed itself. The girls' nice dresses disappeared. In their place came "jeans," real tough jeans. At least, they were intended to convey that effect. Trouser legs carelessly turned up, to keep them out of the mud. But very careful carelessness, kept nicely in place by the maker's precautions. And such spots and daubs of paint all over them, too, the hoydens, such patches—except that the makers had put the patches and the paint on too.

As the sun got warmer, the jeans got fewer, and eventually, the American lasses got down to sun-bathing level, One became quite accustomed to stepping carefully over the serried rows of almost naked American beauties lying on the deck. One can get used to anything I suppose.

One day, a little crowd formed itself about some people in a corner of the boat deck. In my innocence, I supposed it must be some especially interesting exhibition of sun-bathing. In the interest of scientific accuracy, I investigated but discovered that it was a group of heavily clothed people in Spanish peasant costume doing Spanish folk-dancing. A few yards away the naked beauties lay neglected. I was reminded of the story about Lady Godiva and her horse. (It seemed that some time in the distant future Lady Godiva was to ride again. A man was parting from his friend, bound for a neighbouring town. He told him of the ride about to be and suggested he remain to see it. "I believe I will," said the-about-to-depart, "it's a long time since I've seen a horse!")

Half way across we ran into some rough weather. The bow was roped off and the students forbidden to go up into that part of the ship. The bow was immediately covered by students. The captain gave up.

That evening we saw an excellent production of Molière's *Le Médécin malgré lui*. I rather think our French Canadian students were a bit chagrined to find that some of the actors were American students who spoke their lines as well as they themselves could have done.

When a passenger, I keep one little memento of my own days on the bridge, in the form of a pocket mariner's compass—just checking up on the navigation of the ship! It's usually not hard to decide about where one is if he follows courses and distance run. Consequently I "got a little kick out of" predicting to myself when we would see the first light. This duly came in view, the outpost blinker of England on the Scilly Isles. That night, I followed the line of lights ashore, trying to identify the towns. Next day the shores of England advanced and receded as we crossed the wide bights of the south coast. At dawn the morning after, I got up to see what I could see of my old hunting grounds in Dover Straits. The light came too late for me to make out anything but a smudge where Dover itself lay but I had a good nostalgic look at pretty, neat St. Margaret's Bay, where I had spent so many pleasant hours of shore leave and where I had seen my first casualty of the war in the carcase of the destroyer *Nubian,* caught by the enemy in one of their channel raids, left in sinking condition and beached. Then the South Goodwin lightship and, monuments to the insanity of war, a melancholy row of wrecks lying on the Goodwin Sands. The Sands are always claiming their tribute of shipping but in wartime their maw is gorged. Once on, never off.

And after that the placid North Sea all the way across to Rotterdam. Lying in the river of the neat Dutch town, one looked in vain, even then, four years after the war, for signs of war's damage. Not a sign of it. The industrious Dutch had already rescued their port from the indescribable chaos to which it had been reduced and everything was again as it had always been. On one big building the shading of the bricks from the ground floor up was a little lighter in colour than those beneath. That was all!

And then the landing, with 1500 strong young bodies hurtling back and forth, eight hundred in one direction, seven hundred in the opposite. "These American girls don't believe much in privacy," someone said, "they've already got into every hole and corner of the ship. I expect they'll be into our beds before we're through."

They were: but just pre-empting them, while waiting; parking their suitcases and themselves, that's all.

And so, to Europe.